D0628189

VOL. 2

VOL. 2

Open YOUR G.I.F.T.S.

KIM COLES

purposely
created
PUBLISHING

OPEN YOUR G.I.F.T.S., VOL. 2
Published by Purposely Created Publishing Group™

Copyright © 2018 Kim Coles

All rights reserved.

No part of this book may be reproduced, distributed or transmitted in any form by any means, graphic, electronic, or mechanical, including photocopy, recording, taping, or by any information storage or retrieval system, without permission in writing from the publisher, except in the case of reprints in the context of reviews, quotes, or references.

Printed in the United States of America

ISBN: 978-1-948400-80-0

Special discounts are available on bulk quantity purchases by book clubs, associations and special interest groups. For details email: sales@publishyourgift.com or call (888) 949-6228.

For information log on to www.PublishYourGift.com

Table of Contents

Forgiveness

Triumph

Self-Love

Foreword

I'm Reginald McKiver, the husband of Kim Coles. When asked to write the foreword of her latest project, I deemed it as an honor. A chance to eternally submit in writing words that would endure throughout the ages about the woman I love with all of my heart. To be able to amplify her mark through the expression of writing. I support her and every woman who will express their interpretation of G.I.F.T.S.

When I first met Kim, she expressed her interest in G.I.F.T.S. and how she and others would use it to transform the world. She wanted to affect change and, in doing so, wanted to open the door for others to be able to do the same. "Everyone has a gift," she stated, and went on to say, "Who are we? Or anyone, to say that your gift is not important, or would not be life changing for others?" Kim did not want to be defined as an actor and was in the process of reinventing herself to do what she was born to do: spread joy.

Open Your G.I.F.T.S. is a collection of personal stories of triumph through adversity, enlightenment, perseverance, and tenacity—written by women who have embraced their personal power—to bring us together by opening up their souls to help free yours! What I love is that it calls you, the reader, to participate through creating not just a brilliant read, but an experience. Some of these women I know personally, and can attest to their greatness and their desire to be heard in a way that helps others.

Opening your G.I.F.T.S. is a momentum, a movement for such a time as this. By one woman opening her G.I.F.T.S., she has created a way to transfer this gift to another woman, and to another, and now to you. This makes it an energy in which you now become a partaker. No longer are we prisoners and partakers of our own story; we are now free to share our story and to unify. There is power in expression, a power of releasing actions and words that once had you bound, only to discover that your hurt has a dual purpose. That once what could have been set up to destroy you, has now turned into a blessing to the nation. Through this book, may you discover your power, your career changer, and your destiny enhancer.

Let this book, this movement, run. Pass it along to a neighbor, a friend, a sister or brother—anyone who struggles with their G.I.F.T. May it be a blessing to you. It is my prayer that Kim, and the women of these experiences, cause a transformation in your life. Keep this book handy, follow its application, and keep it moving.

It is an honor and a privilege.

Reginald McKiver

Gratitude

Living Grace

Evelyn Ratcliffe

Evelyn Anne, which means Living Grace, was the name I was given at birth. I embarked on a journey of learning and love as we all do in this life, and this is my story.

The quote by Marilyn Monroe "Sometimes good things fall apart so better things can fall together" resonates with me now as I look back on my life experiences. My life has had several occurrences where everything seemed to be falling apart. However, there was a point in my life where it felt like there was no way anything else could have fallen apart. It was a five-year crucible where my life was turned upside down.

I was the sole breadwinner in my family of four—two school-aged daughters, my husband, and me. My husband was out of work with an on-again-off-again back injury. But he was back at work now. Time to get caught up on some bills. I could afford to go back to school, and family vacations were back! I had just wiped my brow and sighed a huge sigh of relief when…

It started with a meeting at work. My company had decided to join many companies at that time, and the whole information technology department was being let go, outsourced to a company in India. I was one of roughly 150 people who would be facing a job hunt directly on the heels of what is now known as the "Great Recession."

Then, the other shoe dropped. I discovered my husband was having an affair. I was sure God had turned His back on me. Our relationship had been rocky for some time, but I was sure it was normal with raising kids and the financial stressors we had with my husband's back injury and subsequent inability to work off and on for about five years. Fast forward, and there was 18 months of marriage counseling followed by a bitter divorce that lasted another 18 months and cost more than $60,000. My home went into foreclosure. I lost my retirement, my cars, and most of my worldly goods, but the greatest hit to my soul was losing my kids. This was the result of the unfortunate combination of teenage judgment and a union-provided lawyer whom I could not afford to fight. Nothing can compare to that. I would never choose to go through that again.

I went from contract position to contract position, each one ending prematurely due to a budget cut, an acquisition not completed, or another reason. My only consolation was that with each of these, my whole team was cut, and I was not singled out. Still, my days were filled with either tears or anger. I missed my children with a pain I can't describe. There was a deep hollow pain in my chest and stomach daily. It was at that time that I had stopped talking to God and doing any soul work.

Then one day, I remembered something I used to do with my children. I may have read about it in the doctor's office when they were small or heard about it passively on a television show. I remembered a vision board. I decided at that moment to do a new one, for no other reason than I needed a distraction and an outlet. My day-to-day life was something from which I needed an emotional escape. My kids and I had fun when we made vision boards. Plus, I love to dream. The result was a spark of hope that was not there before, like a small ember that caught a breeze. A change had started. I was not aware of it then, but that was my fork in the road. I reconnected with my soul's purpose.

**"How you do anything is how you do everything."
—Martha Beck**

I started slowly and unconsciously adding more growth and actives to my life, like drops in a bucket or like a sunflower turning to meet the sun. The small actions added up.

With small, purposeful intentions, I continued to grow and become more hopeful. As my flame of hope started to light my heart, I went from the vision board with setting some goals to realigning myself with what was in my heart and soul. I picked up some books on money and self-esteem. My mind grew clearer, and the cloud of anger and pain grew thinner. I could see past the darkness. Then came self-care and the realization that you cannot pour from an empty vessel. This was a tough one for me—and most mothers, I imagine. We hardly take time to stop and invest in ourselves. We ignore our peace, growth, health, and heart. We see it all the time—a weary mother muttering nonsense due to lack of sleep or poor nutrition as she works tirelessly to support the family.

Fast forward roughly a year. My physical health was better. I suffered fewer migraines. I had gotten a job with some of the loveliest people I had ever met and supportive co-workers and boss. This was an environment of generosity and innovation. I finally felt I was living my life; one which I was comfortable and pleased to call mine. It was not a perfect process, but it was good. My small actions started delivering more than a pile of circumstances beyond my control, where I spent all my time resolving before.

Phoenix Rising - Intentional recovery and healing

> "Your level of success will rarely exceed your level
> of personal development."
> —Jim Rohn

My eyes were opened, and I kept at this growth. I was a Phoenix rising. My birthplace, Phoenix, AZ, is named after the mythical bird, so its symbolism has had a special place in my mind and heart.

Intention can save you from guilt, deliver you from feeling less than, and move you forward during times of hardship and tragedy.

For years, I did not understand intention. Then, I realized that when you are living according to your convictions and believing in something higher than yourself while acting in congruence with your heart and soul, you are living with intention.

At this point, I was setting five-year, annual, and monthly goals, keeping my purpose in front of me as much as I knew how, like a map. I was making annual financial and personal growth plans and tracking my progress on my long-term goals. I had a five-year plan to buy a home. This was a big milestone for me on the path of rebuilding. I called a mortgage broker to do a quick touch-base and see where I needed to focus my next steps to reach that goal. She asked me a few questions, considered a few things, and called me back. I was told I could start shopping for a home and be preapproved in January! This was in October, three years into the five-year plan! My mind was blown. When I started with an intention, put it on paper, and started tracking my goals toward it, life was meeting me halfway. It was closing in the gap to make my goals and dreams come true. When you plant a seed and water it, the life in that seed does the growing. I was seeing this happen in my life with my plans—slow, steady growth when I planted that seed with intention and gave it the regular care and watering of faith, courage, and hope.

"Do the best you can until you know better, then you do better."
—Maya Angelou

I am sure you have heard the phase "intentional living" before, but what is it, really? Why is it important? The first important piece of intention is that much like setting up your GPS to point you to a new store across town or to a friend's home, setting your intentions allows you to align your path with your values and goals rather than following what your friends, family, schoolmates, or even the media hand you. It is about being focused on your goals and actions rather than being blown by the wind. However, your intention could be "to go with the flow." In that case, you will choose to not over-plan and leave room in your life for the "flow moments." If your values align with minimalism, your intentions could line up with less purchasing and collecting of items. An alignment with lifelong learning would result in intentional activities and a lifestyle that supports education. There is no right or wrong. Setting intentions is about what you value and what makes your heart sing.

WHY DOES IT MATTER?

It was at that point that I realized hardly anything is a coincidence when I was also looking for deeper meaning and a connection to my heart and soul. I had looked up the meaning of my name; my name means Living Grace, and it resonated with me. As a result, I have tried to align myself with that meaning. I interpret it as Living, full of vibrancy and joy, and Grace, ease and elegance, like a flower. It grows vibrant and beautiful without a hint of struggle. I look at my responses to situations now and ask myself, "Is this a graceful reply? Is this solution full of vibrancy and life?" These are my markers, my landmarks, for the direction I set my intentions.

How do you build intention into your life? Most of us live on autopilot and take what comes our way. Intention and purpose change the direction of your life from passive to proactive. Victim to victor. The power returns to you in your life. Your circumstances may be out of control, but with intention, you set your rudder to guide your reactions and directions. It is all yours. You are in the pilot seat. Small steps will begin your journey.

First, take some time and see yourself living a life you dream of and relish. Let go of unbelief. What does your day look like—morning, afternoon, and night? Who is there? What do you do? What do you eat? I like to think of it as my dream movie—the story of my dream life.

Next, what are the key themes in your dream life? Mine are honesty, independence, clarity, speaking, solution finding, and humor.

Pause, and without judgment, ask yourself about your current life situation. How is it aligned with your dream life?

What is not matching up to your soul print? What is out of the agreement with your heart, your values, and your dreams? What decisions do you need to make to change the course of your life to steer yourself toward your dream life?

You are in the driver's seat with your intentions. Want to add some real power?

Write out a list of all your current complaints, problems, and things you want to change. I love to make a mind map and group the common themes. My topics could land around money, education, career, relationships, health, and spiritual growth. I was always forgetting to make special care and time for fun. I was too busy to stop and smell the roses.

Now think 10 years out. What does your dream life look like? Draw it on paper, color it with pencils, crayons, or paint, or make a vision board. The point is to do something with your hands—something colorful and creative to activate as many of your senses as possible. Be sure to put a date on it. You are mapping your journey.

To be in that dream in 10 years from today, where would you need to be in five years, one year, six months from today? Place that in your heart.

Today, as I look back on my life, I am filled with more joy than pain. The struggles seemed for nothing when they occurred. However, the past now has a purpose, and it was all for my good and to grow me to my fullest potential. And I am not done! My next steps, my choices in growth, will determine the rest of my path. I could lose it all again, or I could win at this game of life, but I will do all of it according to my soul print. The only thing you can change in your life is where you are right now. We forget that right now is not the end. Your right now is your beginning. Practice small daily steps of intentional acceptance of yourself and where you are now. Add to that practice intentional self-esteem with positive self-talk and blessings. Carve out intentional boundaries in your relationships to focus on where to choose to spend your physical time and mental energy in a positive, uplifting way. We will begin walking in our soul print, as unique as each of us and as unique as each petal on a flower. This is not our end. This is our beginning.

The Foundation for Life

Ruby Mabry

When I think of gratitude, I think of being thankful. I believe the more grateful you are, the more blessings come your way.

For as long as I could remember, my parents would tell me to be thankful for what I had because many people did not have food, clothing, or a place to live. We never wasted food at my house. My parents were immigrants from Haiti, so they were speaking from their personal experience. We always heard about them having one pair of shoes and walking to school every day or how they had to do strenuous chores inside and outside. Not to mention the limited amount of food and number of food options. I realized that we really did have it made, because we had everything in our home that they told us they did not have in Haiti, which made life much easier for us. Hearing of my parents' story was an awakening, because it completely changed my mentality. Even at that young age, it kept me from wasting food and taking things for granted, such as having a place to live and clothes on my back. Many people in the United States complain about what they don't have even though we have it much easier than people in so many other countries. Hearing about my parents' struggles from early on made me appreciate their wanting us to have more and not to suffer the way that they did. I learned that even though we were not lacking anything, there were those who were. Therefore, we should be grateful for everything. This is when my journey to gratefulness spread its wings and took flight. There were four pivotal gratitude moments in my life.

My first real introduction to being grateful was after the birth of my younger brother. My mother went from walking, to her legs dragging, to using a walker, to being confined to a wheelchair. I was still young, and I could not understand why all of this was happening. There were complications with her delivery, and not too long afterwards, she started having complications with walking. Many surgeries later, she was confined to a wheelchair. She did not let that stop her. She still provided for her family, cooked, ironed, cleaned, and did everything she needed to. I would feel sorry for her because she had no use of her legs, but she kept pushing and remained positive. She did everything someone ambulatory could do. I would pray for her in hopes that she would one day walk again. I would talk to myself and God and ask why it was that she could not walk. Why would God do this to her? I saw what my mother would always teach us. She always said to never make fun of people because you never know where life would take you. She was absolutely right. Some of us take for granted being able to use our legs to walk, our mouths to talk, and our eyes to see. We should all be grateful as she was, because at any given moment, it can be taken away from you.

My second pivotal moment was being a military wife at the tender age of 18. You talk about a shift in mindset. Being a military wife made me grow up fast. Civilians, as they call them, do not truly understand the magnitude of what a soldier's day and life is. I remember hearing the stories about boot camp and the struggle and arduous training. Physically, it involved doing sit-ups, push-ups, and obstacle courses and marching in the snow. The mental training involved learning to use survival and tactical skills. It is draining mentally and physically. Trainees are pushed to the limit. After boot camp, I realized that not only did my husband have to get up early for physical training, (PT) as they call it, but I had to get up early as well to make sure breakfast was ready for him when he returned so that he could shower and dress and get ready to go to work in a timely manner. This was repetitive throughout our military career. Yes, I said our, because I served as well, even though I did not go through boot camp. I was putting in work by ironing military creases into his shirts. I was spit-shining boots. I was doing everything to make his stressful life easier. Things totally got real when we went overseas to Germany and the Iraq War was going on. Any time we went on and off base, our vehicle was inspected. A mirror was used to look underneath the vehicle. If anything looked suspicious, the vehicle was searched. We were at great risk. There were so many families without their soldiers due to deployment. I remember my husband was deployed several times while I was pregnant, and I had a high-risk pregnancy. He had to have his friend take me to my appointments while he was away for months at a time. It was stressful to say the least.

During this time, I looked at how stressful, strenuous, and uncertain this whole military situation was, and I opened my eyes to see how dedicated and selfless these soldiers are to sacrifice their lives for our freedom. We take so many things for granted, and our freedom is definitely one of those things. I am grateful every day that my soldier is still here. I remember the days I complained because I was home with our daughter all alone. I remember the days I complained because I could not complete my education due to having to be a full-time Mom while he sacrificed and went to work for us and his country. I remember saying to myself, "Why does the military always come before we do?" There was one point during our first few years in the military when I literally became jealous of the military because it had so much of his attention.

I reflected, stepped back, and came to the realization that many times we feel discouraged, alone, and ungrateful, but we should all realize that freedom is a gift—a gift for which the men in uniform sacrifice their lives every day. Their lives are a gift. Their sacrifice is a gift, and our freedom is a gift. I am so grateful to be free because of them. Anytime I come across any soldier, I thank them not only for their service, but for their selflessness and sacrifice. They spend so much time away from their loved ones, and they deserve the respect and the accolades that come along with serving, wearing their uniform, and all that accompanies it.

I learned to be grateful because the soldiers sacrificed much more than we ever had to sacrifice, and they were doing this all for us. Their time lost with their family is irreplaceable.

My third gratitude journey came from giving birth to my children. I was so fearful with my pregnancies. So many things could happen health wise. With my first-born, I was considered high risk due to my blood pressure. Due to my health risk, my labor was induced with Pitocin, which speeds up the process. My water had to be broken for me with a long wand, and after many hours and painful contractions, my daughter came out healthy and beautiful. We stayed in the hospital seven days after the birth for observation and medical treatment.

With my second child, I was also high risk with preeclampsia, which entails seriously elevated blood pressure and protein in the urine. This pregnancy showed me what the real definition of pain was. My son did not want to come out. It was a long process of pushing, waiting, and trying to flip him due to his positioning. The doctor stated if he did not come out with the next few attempts, I would have to have a cesarean section. The next few contractions came, and I pushed, and he came out. To my surprise, there was no sound. No crying. They whisked him away behind me to work on him. I didn't even get a chance to see him. I immediately started crying, asking what was going on. After what seemed like forever, he started to cry. I was later told he had to be resuscitated because he was not breathing. All of this is to say that there is a higher power, and I am so grateful that even though I went through two high-risk pregnancies, both of my children came out healthy and have been my light in my time of darkness. I am grateful for my faith and scripture during this time. I turned to Proverbs 3:5-8 (NKJV): "Trust in the LORD with all your heart, And lean not on your own understanding; In all your ways acknowledge Him, And He shall direct your paths. Do not be wise in your own eyes; Fear the LORD and depart from evil. It will be health to your flesh, And strength to your bones."

On that part of my journey, I learned to give it all to God because it is out of my hands. I am grateful for two lives that I brought into this world.

My fourth gratitude journey is my health. I have had many surgeries and many close calls with life itself, but God had a greater purpose for me, and I am here to make a change in the world and be used as a vessel to help someone through their struggle and triumph. I am grateful because many are not awarded the opportunity to see another day. I am grateful for being here to minister to others and give back. I am grateful that even though my parents are not here, I was able to help them during their time of illness and take care of them as they did me until their demise. I am grateful for life, a true blessing denied to many. I am alive, blessed, and forever grateful. No matter what I am going through, I try to see the positive and the lesson in it.

Take nothing for granted and always give thanks. Count your blessings and all that is right in your life. Show gratitude and be thankful for all that you already have. The more grateful we are, the more our lives will flourish. The real joy in life is finding gratitude in the simple things every day. This should be our foundation for life.

Single, Black, Male Parent

Sabrina R. Dean, MSA, BSN, RN

I am a black female who has obtained a bachelor's degree in Nursing and a master's degree in Healthcare Administration. I am currently a doctoral candidate for a Healthcare Administration degree. I am a healthcare leader. I was reared by my father, who was a single parent. I was in the bathroom with my dad while he was shaving one day. It looked like fun, so I asked my dad to give me some of his shaving cream. "I am going to shave too," I proudly declared. He said, "Little girl, you can't shave. I am a man." My dad telling me not to shave made me feel sad. I said to myself, "This isn't fair." I felt alone, and I wanted my mommy. I cried.

This was all happening because I really wished I could have watched my mother put on her makeup, but my mother was gone. She had died a year before.

Mother's Day is my least favorite holiday. I don't like to go to church or participate in any of the Mother's Day activities. You see, when I was three years old, my mother passed away from a brain tumor. I don't remember this, but my family told me that she had a sore throat. She kept drinking lots of water, and she couldn't tell the family why. A year and half later, a malignant brain tumor was confirmed, and she died at the age of twenty-four. Unfortunately, I do not have any memory of my mother, but what I do have is lots of female family members who held her memory for me. And of course, I have my dad. I thank God every day for my dad.

My dad, now a widower, was able to raise me and my big brother as a single parent. He decided to keep us instead of placing us into foster care. He provided for my brother and me to the best of his ability. You know how little girls sit at their mothers' feet and watch their mothers put on makeup? Well, I did not have that. I would sit in the mirror and watch my dad shave. I thought I had to shave too. My dad would tell me, "No, no, no. That's not what little girls do." It must have been funny and painful for him at the same time. I'm grateful that my father filled the gaps by contacting the female family members who lovingly explained applying makeup and wearing high heels. In my eyes, my dad was my superhero.

I recall when I was eleven years old and I went to urinate. When I pulled my panties down, I noticed blood in my panties. I screamed out to my dad for him to come into the bathroom. He came into the bathroom, and I showed him the blood in my panties. I told him I thought I had hurt myself. My dad realized what was happening, and he called a female friend who came to the house with sanitary napkins and explained to me about my period. I had not been informed about starting my period and am very thankful for my dad reaching out to his female friend to explain the period process. This was a pivotal life lesson about my gift of gratitude for my dad. My dad helped me to understand an important part of being a woman.

My dad did not do my hair care because he didn't know how. So, he would take me to female family members' homes and to the beauty salon.

To replace the feminine energy in my life, my dad made sure my grandmothers and aunties gave me the feminine qualities I needed. But what my dad does not realize is that the male qualities he gave me serve me to this day. Some people would say I am direct. Some people would say I am always on time. These qualities were given to me by my dad. The bad news is that my dad made me direct, and the good news is that my dad made me direct! At times this has served me well, and at times this has caused issues, but I'm glad for this quality.

My dad taught me the lesson that if I am on time to an appointment, I am already late. As a result, I arrive early to appointments. I am thankful for my dad instilling this quality into me. This quality has served me well, though sometimes I get on people's nerves because I am early all the time!

My dad taught me your word is your word. If you say you are going to do something, then you do it on time. My dad taught me to follow through. As a result of this teaching, I require follow-through of my spouse and friends. I have set a high standard, and those individuals in my circle know to bring their A-game when interacting with me because I bring my A-game for myself.

My dad did not nurture my brother and me, but he took such good care of us, and I have learned to fill my nurturing cup by nurturing others. I have been a Registered Nurse for twenty-two years, and I cared for one of my great aunts who suffered with Alzheimer's until she passed. I was angry as a young girl because I did not have a mother. I became the nurturer that I needed to become for others. I do not nurture myself a lot, but I certainly do nurture the rest of the world.

As a young girl, my pediatrician inspired me to become involved in the medical field. She was the first woman I saw in a leadership role, and I wanted the same for myself. This pediatrician inspired me to obtain my doctorate, which I am currently pursuing.

Even though I don't have my mom, my aunties saved some wonderful pictures of her, which I treasure with my life. These pictures do not replace my mother but are the only memories I have of her. At times, it hurts me to not have known the woman who birthed me. I often wondered what her scent resembled. I would often ask God why He took her away from me. I also realize God needed another angel to help Him.

And as you can tell, I treasure the relationship with my dad.

He did what he could to make me the woman I am today.

I told you in the beginning, I really don't like Mother's Day, but you better darn well believe that I double up on Father's Day! Thank you, Dad, for all that you have done for me.

A scripture that has helped me during this time without my mother is "*It is* good to give thanks to the Lord, And to sing praises to Your name, O Most High; To declare Your lovingkindness in the morning, And Your faithfulness every night." —Psalm 92:1-2 (NKJV)

I Am Grateful for My Parents

Shirley Jean Bazemore

"Honour thy father and thy mother:
that thy days may be long upon the land which
the LORD thy God giveth thee."
—Exodus 20:12 (KJV)

Honoring your father and mother is being respectful in word and action and having an inward attitude of esteem for their position. "Children, obey your parents in everything, for this pleases the Lord" (Colossians 3:20, NIV). Growing up, my parents always reminded us of the importance of being respectful. For this reason, I have the utmost gratitude for my parents.

> "You simply will not be the same person two months from now after consciously giving thanks each day for the abundance that exists in your life. And you will have set in motion an ancient spiritual law: the more grateful you are, the more will be given to you."
> —Sarah Ban Breathnanch

The Positive Psychology Program at Harvard Medical School defines gratitude as "thankful appreciation for what an individual receives, whether tangible or intangible." With gratitude, people acknowledge the goodness in their lives. As we cultivate a grateful attitude, we become happier.

We go through life taking our parents for granted, not realizing how important they are to us. You might think of your parents as being strict, when really they are trying to teach you the difference between right and wrong. My parents were strict with me growing up, and I am thankful. If they had not been strict with me, I would have been reacting on my emotions. It was truly a blessing for me to have grown up with both parents in my life. My parents worked diligently to provide a loving, warm, caring home for their children.

Growing up, my parents taught me the importance of working hard and saving money. I always asked myself why I needed to know about saving money as a child. It was not until I became an adult that I realized the significance of saving money. At the age of 12, my mom had me working on a tobacco farm during the summer months to buy school clothes. My mom told me if I wanted new school clothes, then I had to work. This was the beginning of my taking on responsibility and learning about saving money. Every summer thereafter, I worked on the tobacco farm with my mother. My mother was teaching me how to be responsible. So, Mom, I probably did not tell you back then, but thank you for allowing me to make my own money. Mom, I am grateful for that experience working with you during those summer months.

EARLY MORNING PRAYER

My mom began her day at 5:00 a.m., Monday through Sunday. She did her prayer after waking up in the morning. When we were growing up, she told the children the importance of praying before getting your day started. After prayer, she cooked breakfast for the family. I do not remember my mom ever not making breakfast for the family. When she finished in the kitchen, it was time to read the Bible. Psalm 23 was my mom's favorite Bible scripture:

The LORD is my shepherd; I shall not want.

He maketh me to lie down in green pastures: he leadeth me beside the still waters.

He restoreth my soul: he leadeth me in the paths of righteousness for his name's sake.

Yea, though I walk through the valley of the shadow of death, I will fear no evil: for thou art with me; thy rod and thy staff they comfort me.

Thou preparest a table before me in the presence of mine enemies: thou anointest my head with oil; my cup runneth over.

Surely goodness and mercy shall follow me all the days of my life: and I will dwell in the house of the LORD for ever. (KJV)

Mom, I am grateful for all the mornings you arose to pray for the family and make us breakfast. Mom, I do remember telling myself that one day, I would do the same for my family. Mom, I just wanted to let you know that day has not come yet. I am waiting on God to bless me with a family. Mom, I do my morning prayer, and I still read Psalm 23. The gospel singer Dorothy Norwood's song "Somebody Prayed for Me" is a powerful song. Well, my mom prayed for me, and I am so glad she did. There is power in praying. My mom attended church faithfully, and she carried the children with her. She said, "Shirley, when you get older, you are going to understand why you should attend church." Mom, I am older now, and I do understand that going to church is important. Mom, I am grateful that you were faithful with church. There is a season for everything in your life. We do not always understand the when, but God does. We just have to trust God and surrender all to Him. Looking back over my life, over my past hurts, I could have easily given up; but,

Mom, I am grateful that you were there for me. I am grateful to God for allowing me to have praying parents in my life.

Parents have to endure so many challenges throughout their lives, so be grateful for the smallest things they do in your lifetime. I am grateful that my parents did not allow me to stay out late. I am grateful for the Sunday morning calls when I was in college. So, Mom and Dad, I just wanted to say thank you, and I love you with all my heart. Even though you all are not here to witness your prayers being answered, I know you all are smiling in Heaven. Mom and Dad, I just wanted to let you both know how much I miss you. I am grateful for our laughs we shared together. I am grateful for the times we watched TV together. I am grateful for Bible study together. Dad, remember we watched John Osteen together every Friday night at 7:00 p.m. on TBN? Well, Dad, his son, Joel Osteen, is the head of the church now. Dad, I am grateful you asked me to come and watch TBN with you on Fridays. I think about you when looking at Joel Osteen on TBN.

Reasons Kids Stop Respecting Their Parents

1. Just telling kids their behavior is not okay is not enough. According to a *Psychology Today* article by Erica Reischer, PhD, parents unintentionally let disrespectful behavior continue for several reasons:

2. They are not paying attention to the situation and don't notice the disrespectful behavior.

3. They have gotten used to the behavior.

4. They aren't sure how to change the behavior.

5. The behavior fits their expectation of how kids behave.

Whatever the reason, "allowing" your kids to treat you poorly is establishing a dysfunctional pattern of behavior (aka: a bad habit) and makes it more likely that your kids will treat others that way too. Because children notice both what we say and what we do, we also need to "do" something differently in response to their disrespectful behavior when a reminder isn't sufficient. For example, don't continue the conversation while your child is yelling or speaking disrespectfully. Don't just give up when your child ignores what you are asking to be done. Disrespectful behavior is one of the inappropriate ways kids, especially teenagers, try to solve their problems. It is important for parents to be role models in front of their children. Remember, they are watching you, even if they don't seem like they care what you do. If you value respect from your child, then model respectful behavior. Do your best to show them the way it should be done.

According to Megan Devine, a licensed clinical therapist, kids respond well to praise. Not only does it feel good to be praised, it gives your child important feedback. Acknowledging good behavior reinforces those skills. Let your children know you appreciate them.

You can't demand respect, but you can require that your child acts respectfully no matter how they feel about a situation.

Parents need to have conversations with their children. Ask who, what, when, where, why, and how questions to find out what's happening inside of your child's mind. Parents can always teach their children about prayer. I am grateful my parents prayed in front of me. I am grateful my parents showed me the value of life. If you want something in life, you have to be willing to work hard and have faith in God. In my opinion, this principle of life still operates in today's society. It is important to attend school and college to get your education. "In everything you do, put God first, and he will direct you and crown your efforts with success" (Proverbs 3:6, TLB).

My brother and sisters did not even think about disrespecting our parents. We witnessed how diligently our parents worked to provide for us. When I was told "no" as a child, my parents gave me a good reason for their decision.

Mom and Dad, I know you both are enjoying Heaven, and I wanted to tell you that I think about you all every day. Life has been a challenge for me since you all were called home to Heaven.

I decided to write about you both in remembrance of the love you shared with your family. I thank God for blessed parents. You all did an excellent job raising seven children. We are doing well for ourselves. Thank you both for paying for my education. Mom, I am fulfilling one of my goals you and I talked about from time to time. Your prayers are still being answered even though you are not here on Earth. You both live on in our hearts. I will see you both one day, and our laughs will begin again.

"And now abideth faith, hope, charity, these three; but the greatest of these is charity."—1 Corinthians 13:13 (KJV)

I love you, Mom and Dad, forever!

"Gratitude can transform common days into thanksgivings, turn routine jobs into joy, and change ordinary opportunities into blessings."
—William Arthur Ward

Surviving Through It All

Tammie Kincaid

In life, we don't get to choose how things end, especially when you have the "Happily Ever After" vision for your marriage. That vision ended abruptly after my amazing husband lost his hard-fought second battle to cancer on December 3, 2016, which was also the day that our oldest son, Dylan, turned 4 years old. I'm thankful that he held on until his birthday. I try to look at the bright side of things. In this case, I will be busy planning a birthday party, which will keep me from being too sad leading up to the anniversary of Kevin's death each year. The gift of gratitude stands out the most because despite everything that I went through when I faced cancer twice and then a decade later when my husband faced cancer, I am thankful for the amazing friends, family, co-workers, sorority sisters, college friends, church members, neighbors, and strangers whom God placed in our lives along the way to help us through it all.

The night of the conference call to receive information about *Open Your G.I.F.T.S., Volume II*, I decided to stop by the cemetery to visit my late husband's gravesite after I left the car dealership. It's amazing how God works and how things are aligned. I've seen it many times over my 39 years here on Earth; however, I've seen it more so since Kevin passed away. After I decided where I wanted to have my husband buried, I realized that it was near the car dealership. I had passed the cemetery various times over the last two years, but never paid much attention to it. Little did I know that I would later have many visits there each time I went to the car dealership and on my way home after 11 out of the 12-week sessions of group grief counseling class I attended.

The reason why I went to the car dealership was because I lost a second set of keys to my car and house after Kevin passed away. It's amazing how much you forget, lose things, and lose focus after the loss of a loved one. After my keys were missing for about two weeks, I decided to have my late husband's SUV towed to the car dealership and get another set of keys made. Thank God that I did, because two days later, my youngest son broke his left femur bone at the daycare. My oldest son's former daycare teacher was scheduled to babysit that evening because I normally attended my weekly women's Bible study group. We didn't meet, so I scheduled a massage, which was one of the things that I did along with getting manicures and pedicures and taking trips with family, friends, and my sorors to help me through the grieving process after Kevin died. Needless to say, I called and cancelled the appointment for my massage. After picking Logan up from the daycare and putting him in his brother's car seat, I was in a rush to get to the hospital. But I stopped at home, for which I again thank God, and left the key to the other vehicle. Some people questioned why I needed or decided to keep two vehicles after Kevin passed away. Well, my decision to do so helped me that night. I put my hazard lights on and drove on the shoulder lane on the interstate going 80 miles per hour to get to the children's hospital. My need to show gratitude continued because neither my parents nor Kevin's parents lived in Georgia, but I still had their help and support. Logan's godmother and Kevin's friend's wife came to the hospital to bring food and help me with Logan. His friend's wife later helped me after Logan was discharged the next day. I came home to food from one of the ladies from my Bible study group. Another lady dropped off food the next day, and then the group bought a gift for Dylan's birthday, just like many people did when Kevin went through cancer. Again, people came to help me during the five weeks that Logan was in a cast. That was a trying experience with all of the assistance and attention that he required, but it kept me busy and my mind off of the one-year anniversary of Kevin's death, which was closely approaching.

There were many things that Kevin told me during his last year of life. About two weeks before he passed, he told me something that stood out to me, which was to continue to help others. We knew that we were blessed by so many people who helped us along the way. We liked to help others and give back to the community and strangers. About one week before Kevin passed away, we were at our house on Thanksgiving. My nephew, who attends my alma mater, started to question his future ability to be successful as a young African American man due to the many things that were happening to African American males. The guys at the house, including Kevin, tried to uplift him. Kevin wrote a check and gave it to my nephew. Since his passing, I have given away five scholarships to high school and college students. In 2017, I also helped others in need and not in need because I was grateful for the support that we received when we both went through cancer.

When Kevin was alive, we added each other to our calendars on our cell phones. In normal fashion, I added Kevin to my calendar when I scheduled my six-month appointment to see my oncologist. Little did I know, he wouldn't be alive when I had my appointment. He was there for me during both battles that I fought with cancer. I survived them with minimal issues other than chemo, radiation, and surgeries in 2004 and 2006, which are stories in and of themselves. One of the hardest things for me to conceive was the fact that I went "through" and survived cancer, not once, but twice; yet, my husband, the love of my life, would later die from it. In questioning God and wondering why He allowed this to happen to me, I realized one of many things. I knew that He liked to use me, and He continues to do so. He allowed me to survive cancer twice with Kevin by my side so that I could be there for him when he went through chemo, radiation, multiple stays at the hospital (which each lasted from several days to five), and home hospice. All so that I could be right by his side when he took his last breath.

Kevin always wanted me to share my story of my battle with cancer by writing a book. However, life kept happening, and I allowed a plethora of distractions and circumstances to get in the way each time that I would add more to my book. The day that this chapter was due, I made a major decision for myself and the boys. The next day, which was a year after the viewing of Kevin's body, I took a selfie while I was outside playing in the snow with the boys. I thought about the fact that Kevin wasn't here with us to see and experience the first snowfall of the season. Logan, who's almost three years old, wanted me to take a picture of the snowman to show his daddy. It's obviously still hard for him to grasp and understand the concept that his daddy isn't here. Later that day, my cousin saw my selfie and said that she saw peace in my face. That made me feel good, especially since I've had trouble getting a good night's rest since Kevin died. I'm thankful for the snow that kept me from getting down the weekend of the anniversary of his home-going service. The night that I worked on my chapter was literally a year after we said our final farewells to Kevin. Again, it's amazing how God aligns things. He knows the plans that He has for us.

I'm thankful for the opportunity to share my experience as a two-time cancer survivor, widow, and survivor of life in *Open Your G.I.F.T.S., Volume II*. God has given me many gifts, one of which is speaking. The other one is writing, and I can write just as much as I talk. Writing has been one of the things with which I have been blessed, and I am now sharing it in a broader fashion while reaching a larger audience. Show gratitude to those who have helped you along the way. Remember, we all have gifts. Take advantage of yours while you're living, not only to help yourself, but to help others too.

Finding Peace on the Other Side of Obedience

Bob Rodgers

GIFT:
GRATITUDE

Gifts. Calling. Passion. Purpose.

These four words are at the heart of what it means to be human. I believe that as men and women made in the image of God, we all deep down want to know what we're good at—our gifts—and how best to use them on this journey called life. And while most of us want to spend our short time on this earth doing something we're passionate about—and fulfill some sort of higher purpose—figuring out exactly how our gifts and calling fit into the equation often involves trials and tribulations that strengthen us and show us the way.

For me, it took a medical crisis followed by an unfortunate financial decision to be humbled to a point where I could clearly see my greatest gift—gratitude—and fully understand how it energizes my calling and passion to carry out my God-given purpose. Along the way, I learned that gratitude not only unlocks the fullness of life, but it's the key component for joy and a peace that passes all understanding.

You see, in my early 30s, I was running a large and successful division at a company in which I was responsible for more than 22,000 employees in 21 states. My wife and I were having our children, and I repeatedly said that I wanted to be a good dad who would be a significant part of their lives. In reality, however, I wasn't walking my talk. Most work weeks, I left the house on Monday and returned home on Friday or Saturday. It was in this context that my wife and I decided that I would pursue a different career—because we get do-overs when it comes to careers, but not when it comes to kids and a family.

So, I left my successful position and started a job that allowed me to be present for my family. And while success quickly followed in this new position, everything came crashing down one day when the room started spinning as I talked to a colleague on the phone. The initial fear was that I was having a heart attack. But eventually, the doctors decided that I had an inner ear disorder causing vertigo and progressive hearing loss coupled with severe tinnitus. Needless to say, I was shocked when the doctor looked me in the eye and said, "This won't kill you, but it will ruin the rest of your life."

To say that this medical crisis was disruptive is an understatement. As a hard-charging, take-no-prisoners, profit-focused, 34-year-old businessman on the brink of a second successful career, I suddenly found that I really didn't like myself very much. And I realized that if my own voice was going to be the last I hear after I go deaf, I needed to sort some things out.

So, I embarked upon a journey with the help of a licensed professional counselor who saw that my anxiety and self-loathing had a deep spiritual component. In our first session, he asked me a simple question that cut to the core of my Christian faith: "If God wanted to overwhelm you with His love right now—so that you would know and experience how much He deeply loves and cares for you—would you know how to receive it?"

Flabbergasted, I really didn't know what to say. Sure, I understood that God loved me and that He died for me—along with every other person who ever lived—but, I pointed to my heart and said that I didn't think that I understood that He loves me uniquely and individually.

It was from this starting point that my faith in Jesus deepened as I came to understand that God was entirely relational. He died for me personally, cares for me personally, is interested in me personally, and loves me personally. This changed everything. And it unlocked the gift of gratitude in my heart—a gift that would translate into a heart to serve others.

Despite this breakthrough, however, God wasn't finished refining me yet. My natural tendency is to rely on my own strength and abilities and to do things my way and not God's. I had long been motivated to be in a financial position by the time I turned 50 to retire and spend the rest of my life helping people ensnared in sex trafficking and/or sexual exploitation. The pain, hopelessness, and brokenness that drive men and women to turn sexuality into a commodity for sale grieved me, and I knew this dehumanization also grieved God's heart. So, my desire was to get involved in efforts to restore hope as well as offer healing and restoration to those victimized by this evil.

In my mid-40s, however, even this seemingly noble dream was shattered. I made a couple of financial decisions that resulted in my family losing everything—our business, our house, our car, and my financial goals and dreams, it seemed. Yet even in the midst of this economic disaster—one in which I felt like I was a complete failure as a father and husband—God had plans to move forward on His terms and not mine.

Soon, I was the president of a distinguished graduate university. Here, our family learned how to live on far less than I thought possible. Our university added counseling centers and mental health trauma centers in Chattanooga and Atlanta. In due course, we were doing 24,000+ counseling sessions annually, and sexual trauma and abuse issues became more prominent. Our graduates and therapists were sponsoring conferences on human trafficking, doing trainings, working with organizations nationwide to raise awareness on the issue, and building coalitions to combat it at the local, state, and national levels. I was grateful that God was allowing me to make a positive impact on an issue I was passionate about.

But this position only scratched the itch for me. Soon, I felt God leading me to resign my position as university president and move more directly into the sex-trafficking space. Many said, "People don't leave positions like this to do 'that.'" Yet in 2016, I cofounded the Freedom Coalition to bring together organizations in Atlanta fighting trafficking and accepted the position as President and CEO of Street Grace, a not-for-profit that is effectively combating domestic minor sex trafficking throughout the US.

Today, I am grateful for the medical diagnosis that caused me to reflect on the value of my life and health and start living with integrity in alignment with my gifts, calling, passion, and purpose. And though I wouldn't wish it on anybody, I'm thankful for what came out of losing everything financially. Living on a greatly reduced salary helped me realize that there are better ways to "keep score." For me, working to help survivors of sexual exploitation, abuse, and trafficking, educating young people on the issue, and partnering with churches to bring restoration and healing in this area is the "better way."

Most importantly, my heart is filled with gratitude and joy working with people who have overcome things that are beyond my ability to comprehend yet now stand up and smile knowing that God is at work in their lives turning a bad situation into a beautiful, redemptive story. It is their lives that reflect the power of the Gospel to transform and restore. It is their stories that are worth honoring and celebrating.

Here, the inspiring words of one of my favorite Christian authors, John Ortberg, come to mind: "If you want to do the work of God, pay attention to people. Notice them. Especially the people no one else notices."

It is gratefulness that propels me forward and translates into service to others. And while this doesn't mean that everybody should quit their job and work for a nonprofit in order to serve others and exercise their gifts, I do believe that gratitude calls us to examine how we approach our personal calling and passion and ultimately impacts how we live out our purpose to help make the world a better place.

I used to think that being financially "secure" enough to quit everything and help others would make me a good and noble person. And that was my goal. Now I realize just how selfish this view is, because what I was really saying was if I'm financially secure and don't have to sacrifice anything—and all my needs are met—then I'll go and help other people.

Yet, through my journey with the gift of gratitude, I've learned that if serving others is the most important thing, then I should do it regardless. And I've learned to trust the process, be diligent on the journey, and understand that true peace always resides on the other side of obedience—to God and His calling on our lives.

Intention

Learning to Fly (Despite Those Who Would Clip Your Wings)

Claudia Wair

I've known I wanted to be a writer since second grade when I wrote my first poem for a school assignment. But on the first day at my all-girls high school, my plans to be a writer hit a brick wall. I was excited about taking English; it had always been my favorite subject, and I'd already read several of the books on the syllabus. As I left the classroom, my new teacher, Mrs. Smith, stopped me.

"I want you to know you're going to fail this class," she said.

All I could do was stare at her. I didn't have the greatest self-esteem, but one thing I knew was English was my best subject.

Mrs. Smith continued, "You blacks can never write well. The best you can get is a D." She went back into the classroom and closed the door.

I walked to my next class shocked, hurt, and angry. It wasn't my first experience with racism, but it was the first time that someone charged with my education was so explicitly prejudiced.

Later that day, Mrs. Jones stopped me before I could even enter her history class. "Black girls don't do well in history," she said. (It wasn't until much later that I saw the irony in this.) "You're going to fail." She had a satisfied grin as she turned to re-enter the room.

Now I was furious. And determined to prove these people wrong. It was as if I were a small bird and they were trying to clip my wings before I even had the chance to learn to fly.

But…

What if they were right? What if I *wasn't* good enough? I quickly pushed that doubt aside. Nevertheless, it crept into my thoughts again and again.

I worked my butt off that year. With English papers being so subjective, I knew I wouldn't have much of a chance in Mrs. Smith's class. But I aced every single pop quiz and grammar test that woman threw at us and eked out a C. By the end of the semester, I had an A in history. At the last minute, Mrs. Jones assigned a paper. She gave me an F, bringing my grade down to a B. Still, I did better than either of those teachers predicted. I suspect they wanted to dissuade me from even trying.

When my senior year arrived, my college counselor tried to convince me that the school I wanted to attend wouldn't accept me. He tried to get me to apply only to my safety schools, and even "mislaid" some of my paperwork. Fortunately, I knew my grades and test scores were good enough, and with encouragement from other educators, I applied to and was accepted by the college of my choice, one of the best schools in the country.

The abuse I suffered under people who were supposed to teach me stuck with me, making me vulnerable to the Mrs. Smiths and Mrs. Joneses of the world. But their voices were sometimes drowned out by other, more caring voices of teachers, friends, and family. They kept me going until I could hear my own voice say, "You *know* you can do this!" and believe it.

Fifteen years after graduating, I knew I'd proven my detractors wrong when my first publication came out. It was, aptly, the history of a government education program. I watched with pride as it was handed to members of the family of the US president who started that program.

I thought about writing to tell my former teachers about my accomplishment, but decided they weren't worth the effort.

I received my undergraduate and graduate degrees in English. I've been truly blessed to have worked in my field of study for my entire career. Still, the goal of publishing my fiction drifted away. The challenges of everyday life took over, and I told myself that pursuing my dream was frivolous.

Then, a month before my 48th. birthday, I caught pneumonia. During the worst of it, I slept up to 21 hours a day. For some reason, during those three feverish hours awake in the middle of the night, I found myself watching YouTube videos. I stumbled upon one by a woman my age who stepped out of her comfort zone and tried something new—something she'd always wanted to do but never had the courage to try.

When I recovered from my brief illness, I looked at myself in the mirror and said, "No excuses." I didn't want to look back at my life and say I never even attempted to reach this long-held goal.

I needed guidance. I took an inexpensive novel writing course, began entering fiction contests, and got feedback from peers and professionals who offered free critiques.

Less than a year later, my first short story was published.

It wasn't easy. I had my share of missteps and failures. To reach my goal, I had to develop some mental and practical disciplines to improve my focus, manage my time, and disregard the naysayers, including my own nagging self-doubt. As I grew in self-awareness, I learned four important lessons:

1. Create a positive mindset. When things get rough, my reflex is to turn to negative thinking. I had to develop a habit of turning those thoughts around in order to set myself up for success. You must be your own best cheerleader.

The most powerful discipline I practiced was using a daily gratitude journal. It was difficult to start at first; I was in the midst of a deep depression at the time, and it seemed none of my clouds had silver linings. But I forced the issue and started with the basics:

1. I have a roof over my head.
2. I was able to pay (most of) my bills.
3. I have books.
4. There's ice cream in the freezer.
5. My mom loves me.

Every day, write down five things for which you're thankful. You'll be amazed at how it changes your outlook.

2. Do something toward your goal every day. Or at least on a regularly scheduled basis. Even if it's a small thing, it's still a step in the right direction. Keep your steps manageable; when you fail to complete all the tasks on an enormous to-do list, you end up feeling like a failure and might even give up. Schedule this time. Put it on your calendar. When I started, I set a minimum of writing 500 words a day—a small but attainable step.

Be persistent. Try. You might fail, so try again. You'll have learned something.

If you miss a day, don't beat yourself up. Be gentle with yourself! But, be determined as well.

3. Don't allow other voices to deter or distract you.
Even though I survived terrible teachers and came out on the other side triumphant, a part of me still felt haunted by the experiences. A pattern of negativity kept me from fully committing to my aspirations. Either my own inner critic stopped me, or outside voices discouraged and sometimes sabotaged me.

Even people who love us can feel the need to redirect our focus. I wanted to major in English, but my parents wanted me to go into computers. They were thinking about my financial well-being, as good parents do.

Block out those voices. It's *your* life. This is *your* choice. Choose to listen only to encouragement, even if it's your own cheerleading. Create a mantra, a short phrase to repeat to yourself throughout the day, that encourages and uplifts. One of mine was, "Breathe in creativity and calm. Breathe out anxiety."

4. Surround yourself with people who lift you up.
Earlier I said you must be your own best cheerleader. But it certainly helps when you have other people cheering you on. Make sure they're the *right* people.

I had to let go of a friendship that wasn't good for me. It was a particularly difficult time, and the friend just pulled me deeper into a negative space. I felt powerless to uphold necessary boundaries, and my friendship with her got in the way of other relationships. It took me more than a year to get up the courage to step away, but once I did, I was able to navigate to a much better place.

Rekindling relationships with the people I'd neglected during this friendship lifted me almost immediately, and I began writing again.

The world can throw all manner of obstacles in our paths. Negative and even cruel people can try to hold us back. It can be difficult to stay motivated or to maintain confidence in our abilities. But wherever you find yourself along your journey, practice maintaining a positive mindset, take small steps toward your goal, disregard the naysayers, and surround yourself with those who lift you up. Then, no matter who tries to clip your wings, you'll find that you're still able to fly.

Persevering Beyond the Crown

Laura Bella

Struggles, triumphs, challenges, defeat, and accomplishments have all colored my life, and the common denominator of all of my accomplishments comes down to perseverance.

I had a fairly normal childhood. However, at age 15, my life took a turn when I attempted suicide. I didn't want to take my own life. It was, simply put, a desperate cry for help.

From that age and into my late 20s, I was going through the motions, walking around numb, and using food as a vice to comfort me. Not much of an existence. I didn't yet know what my purpose was or where or how I fit in. I was good at many things, however, I never really felt like I found my place, my calling, my purpose. Can you relate?

Finally, I looked in the mirror and really saw myself, and I wasn't happy with my reflection. How had I allowed my life to get so out of control that I had reached nearly 300 pounds?

I felt called for something greater and finally took a stand for me and my life and began the weight loss journey. I'd been on this road most of my life, however, this time I was committed to success.

Shortly after releasing about 120 pounds, I was getting approached to model. I discovered the Miss Plus America Organization, was first named Ms. Plus Illinois, and then went on to compete at Nationals. As I was new to pageant competitions and my intention was to win, I hired a coach. I then went into the studio to record my first Affirmations CD, *"Leadership Affirmations."* This CD was a gift for the reigning queens and delegates. Fortunately, this CD and a few others are currently sold to the public all over the world. I also recorded a personal version just for me with the affirmation "I am Ms. Plus America 2006" so that I could program my brain to believe that I was taking home the crown. I had been trained for years through books and coaches on the power of suggestion and positive affirmations, so I knew firsthand how powerful they can be to the subconscious and conscious mind. I heard "I am Ms. Plus America 2006" over and over again for the three weeks preceding the pageant. I nailed the interview because I spoke from my heart with conviction and was coached on how to intentionally showcase my greatest light. Onto the formal wear competition. I walked the stage as if I already claimed the crown. It was down to the Top 5, then it was Ms. California and me left standing in the top two. "The new Ms. Plus America is Laura Bella!" My mom later said she nearly fell out of her seat. This daughter of hers who had heard, "Laura is so pretty, if only she lost weight" her whole life now won a national beauty pageant. Wow! The next year was a bit of a whirlwind with photo shoots, interviews, speaking engagements, and appearances all over the country.

A few months into my reign, I decided to take it to another level and was selected to compete on the USA team for the World Championship of Performing Arts ("WCOPA") amongst 70 countries. I trained and was coached in modeling, acting, and singing leading to competition. I competed in nine competitions and took home six medals: three golds, two silvers, and a bronze. The craziest part was winning a gold medal in Plus Model Swimwear. This was a huge deal because even though I looked beautiful in my swimwear ensemble, parading it on a stage with confidence and a smile amongst nations and in front of thousands of people and judges was no easy feat. All of the sudden, this amateur model and beauty queen had an agent and a manager and was meeting with top agencies in Los Angeles. I thought these meet-and-greet interviews would be a breeze; I had the smile, the crown, the medals, and the connections. Well, rejection after rejection really took a toll on me, and I started looking for solutions to handle the "not interested." Self-development books, seminars, coaches, and personal development workshops became my new addiction in a healthy way. This began an ongoing 10-plus-year journey of discovery and working through the root cause of how I became nearly 300 pounds. How to handle rejection, learn and grow from it, and come back that much stronger and confident became my new motto on how to handle challenges. How to fall in love with myself over and over again in every moment even through defeat, rejection, sadness, loneliness, and simply every precious moment became my mission.

As I traveled the country as Ms. Plus America and WCOPA Champion, I looked around and noticed that I wasn't alone on this journey of self-love; that a lot of people are hurting and looking for answers on how to love themselves more deeply (or even love themselves at all). The more I learned, the more I became aware of the challenge. This became a passionate calling for my life, the way I would serve the world. I fell in love with my new life.

As I became a self-love subject matter expert, I started thinking of ways I could help others in the hopes that perhaps they could learn a bit faster than I on how to love themselves in order to share that love with others and ultimately feel fulfilled. I created *Laura Bella International* ("LBI"), where we strive to enrich and empower the lives of others with self-love at the core. We start with the true you to discover your baseline and partner together as we coach you to uncover what's needed to take your life to the next level. While this is all in process, we'll collaborate on your goals to understand whatever is needed regarding your relationships—relationship with money, finance, and wealth; relationship with others; and most importantly, relationship with self. At LBI, we partner with our clients by guiding them on their journey in order to bring out their greatness and transform their lives, so they can truly leave the legacy they are meant to.

We are all a work in progress. Every moment is a choice for an opportunity to fall more deeply in love with who you are. Know that the gifts you have to bring are needed in this world, and that is why you're here. Fulfill your passions and live the life of your dreams to leave a true legacy. Overcoming obstacles in life doesn't have to be a struggle, and if it is, then there are people out there like me who have been there who can help you get through it with a bit of ease.

What would your life look like if you awoke every day with a smile, an excitement for your life and those you get to serve every day? What would it feel like to look in the mirror and love and appreciate the reflection you see? What could you create if you knew that failure wasn't an option and that preserving is the best way to get up each time you think you have a failure or a challenge that seems impossible to overcome? How great could life be with a coach, a champion, and a team in your corner to ensure you succeed in creating the life of your dreams? A coach can guide you on how to love yourself and teach you how to be grateful for exactly where you are and excited for the direction you're heading. They can provide you with tools that uncover the truth, which is that everything you have in your life (and don't have in your life) is because of your own design. They can assist you to shift your thoughts and actions so that you begin to attract and create all of the things you truly desire. The sooner you learn how to love yourself, the sooner you can gloriously step into your purpose and a life with which you're so in love.

Get Crazy with YES

Millicent Martin Poole

GIFT:
INTENTION

My house is silent. Still. An occasional breeze from the ceiling vent blows icy air over my left shoulder as I lay prostrate on my home office floor with my nose pressed into the natural-tone carpet, inhaling dusty fibers.

I am paralyzed by back pain with no one to help me.

My husband is at work. My daughters are at school.

If only I could crawl up, gingerly grip each bookshelf, steel my legs, and bring myself to a standing position. The inner gladiator in me tries mind over body, but each time I lift my leg or flinch, a bolt of lightning shoots through my lower back.

So, I am glued to the floor. Cold. And more icy air blows.

How did I get here?

I am embarrassed, as if someone else is in the house, hearing the words inside my brain.

WANTING MORE

Have you ever felt paralyzed, whether by fear, a person, past mistakes, excessive planning, or just second-guessing yourself?

Perhaps you're paralyzed in a career where you long for professional success and personal fulfillment, knowing you're capable of being and accomplishing more, but fear of taking a risk with no guarantee for success keeps you glued to the same level in life.

Maybe you've suddenly gained thirty pounds, accumulated a mountain of debt, filed for divorce, or been diagnosed with an illness. Without noticing the weeks, months, or the signs pass you by, you ask yourself, "How did I get here?"

"This is as good as it will get" or "I'm stuck here" can become a self-fulfilling prophecy.

Lying on my office floor gave me time to reflect on what led me to that point. Was it the marathon hours of sitting at work, pretending everything was fine when, in fact, my job was sucking the life out of me? Did this all land me on the floor, whiffing carpet fibers in my home office?

At that time, I was in accounting, and I had served on the national accounting board for a professional accounting association, consulted business executives, and could do my job in my sleep.

I was successful, but I wanted more.

While paralyzed on my office floor, my second thought was, "I'm too old for this."

I'm not kidding.

I was so burned out and frustrated from helping others climb their respective corporate ladders of success that I'd forgotten to climb it myself. And that was bittersweet and sad. I *enjoyed* helping others develop their gifts and pursue their professional success, but I minimized my own gifts and covered my inner genius.

THE TURNING POINT

My transformation began with a private challenge: What if I listened only to God's instructions over my own wisdom or that of others?

Recovering from my back procedure and physical therapy marked the beginning of my quest to being intentional, standing up for myself, and closing the gap between the life I was living and the life I really wanted.

I called it my YES Journey.

My favorite quote is from Sheryl Sandberg's book, *Lean In*: "Opportunities are rarely offered; they're seized." And my mantra is "Say yes and figure out the details later." If you have ever experienced the paralysis of analysis, this is terrifying and freeing.

I began saying yes, even at the risk of failing. Some yeses came with excruciating pain while others came by surprise, coming out of my mouth faster and faster.

As I prayed more, I began to notice things I'd never noticed before: divine opportunities. The more I moved toward the opportunities, the more doors swung open, and the more exciting my life became. The craziness started shortly after I spoke at a local women's event. That's when God pressed on my heart to write a book.

Me? Write a book? Writing a book makes me nervous, uncomfortable; it will expose my soul to the world!

Being comfortable is what landed me on my office floor. I was comfortable and unfulfilled in my career. Plus, scared.

I Said Yes

I tried keeping myself busy to avoid writing, hoping God would forget or I would forget. He didn't forget. I repented and said yes. This response later morphed into an adventure, unearthing hidden gifts within me. While writing *What Are You Really Running From?* God nudged me to establish a nonprofit organization.

Wait.

A what?

Establishing a nonprofit required money and paying a professional to file a 501(c)(3) application with the IRS. But to my surprise, God wanted *me* to apply despite my lack of experience.

I said yes anyway, and then the miracle happened. Eight months later, my application was approved.

I realized then that to see bigger dreams and miracles happen required stretching my faith. Some call it "walking on water" or "taking a leap of faith." I call it getting crazy with saying yes to God.

I KEPT SAYING YES

One of my boldest prayers happened when I decided to give God complete control of my career. After all, I had invested four years of college, two years in grad school, tuition, and years of building my accounting career. How did I get to this point?

I was just… desperate.

Something had to change. It *had* to because I couldn't imagine the life I was living was it.

That's when I prayed a life-changing prayer: "Not my will, but Thine be done." And as I pressed into His presence, seeking His will, I experienced God like never before and grew addicted to saying yes. Nothing excited me more than seeing how far I could go in life with saying yes.

Author Mark Batterson once stated, "Most of us are educated way beyond the level of our obedience." Well, my test of obedience and achieving a bigger dream came four years later when I said yes to leaving my comfortable accounting career to start my own corporate training company.

Yes, I paid off my debt and left my accounting career. I let it flatline right there before my eyes and walked away into the sunset, like John Wayne, to start my new company. I was ready to break through my personal glass ceiling, make that ceiling my new floor, and evolve into a higher version of myself.

As opportunities arrived in my inbox, I sensed they were divine opportunities and seized them! I challenged my self-imposed limitations while helping others challenge theirs.

I said yes to speaking at conferences, women's retreats, and luncheons and yes to video shoots and studio recordings.

I said yes to becoming a Bible professor and to cold-calling and interviewing female CEOs of multi-million-dollar companies.

I said yes to writing my second book, *Be the Answer NOW*, an Amazon bestseller.

And when I finally allowed myself to be fully seen, laying down my excuses and justifications, I said yes to interviews on national podcasts, radio stations, and TV shows.

This avalanche of yeses led me to becoming a training executive to employees across the US, Mexico, and Canada.

And maybe best of all, a recent yes led me to becoming a co-author with a respected and well-loved actress—and my favorite female comedian—Kim Coles. Yes! Yes!

What Will You Say?

How many opportunities have you talked yourself out of by defaulting to no?

When presented with a divine opportunity, do you delay your decision because of indecision, or do you seize the moment? At some point, you must decide to speak up for yourself and say yes to God. Get crazy with it!

What's the secret to standing in the sun and finding the courage to go after the life you really want?

Trusting God and trusting yourself. Forcing yourself to do what scares you, taking risks, and pursuing your goals with gusto! Ultimately, it's having an insatiable desire to explore, applaud, and embrace your uniqueness. Loving your truest self.

How far are you willing to go to see a higher version of you? Don't say yes to a divine opportunity while looking for an exit door. Don't put on the brakes. *Accelerate.*

Saying yes changed my life and it will change yours too.

Getting crazy with yes has taken me places I've only dreamed of and allowed to work with people I could never have imagined working with and to inspire others to be intentional and change their lives by saying one little word: YES.

So, what will you say?

A Prescription for Intentional Living

Dr. Jamie Hardy, The Lifestyle Pharmacist®

Don't let the white coat fool you. The doctorate degree and professional accolades do not automatically qualify me as having it all together. In fact, what they do is create expectations from family, friends, and society of what my life should look like. Every aspect of my life—from the brand of clothes and shoes I wear to the handbags I carry—has been dissected by others. Let's not leave out the type of car I drive, the square footage of my home, the places I vacation, and last but not least, my job. That last one has been my biggest struggle and the cause of the most heated discussions with the people closest to me. Yes. I followed the formula—go to school, make good grades, attend a great college, get a well-paying job to create a comfortable life for myself. But something was missing.

From the day that I was accepted into pharmacy school, the entrepreneurial fire burning inside of me refused to be extinguished. I knew that I wanted to own a business of my own. The problem was that I did not know how to leverage my pharmacy knowledge and training to create a successful and profitable business. As a result, I opened and closed four businesses within a six-year period. I had a boutique event planning company, I flipped houses, I had a travel agency, and I even sold premium hair extensions. To put it mildly, I was an unsuccessful serial entrepreneur. Don't get it twisted. My failed business attempts were not due to a lack of hard work or poor planning, but because I was refusing to embrace my purpose. I was running from the very thing that I had been placed on this earth and called by God to do—change the world one person at a time by teaching people how to make intentional daily changes in their lifestyle. You see, I survived major depression and thoughts of suicide by changing my eating habits, exercising, and meditating. Food became my medicine, exercise became my daily therapy, and meditation became my source of peace. I intentionally made over my lifestyle, and those changes literally saved my life! Now I am a board-certified pharmacist, bestselling author, media personality, and medical expert who helps people who are busy juggling businesses, relationships, and careers to be fit, fabulous, and fulfilled without prescribed pills. Through my videos, books, and programs, they learn how to detox, eat healthier, effectively manage stress, and incorporate physical activity into their fast-paced lives so that they can live the life of their dreams.

I am a practicing clinical pharmacist in Memphis, Tennessee. I realized that I needed to tap into my gift when I continued to encounter patients, relatives, and church members being repeatedly admitted to the hospital because of a crisis in their health. Many of them were taking over 10 prescription medications each day for conditions like diabetes, high blood pressure, high cholesterol, kidney failure, and heart disease. Yes, it is my job to be their pharmacist—to review their medication list for appropriate doses, check for drug interactions, and identify any side effects they were experiencing. The issue was that I wanted to offer more than a temporary Band-Aid to their problem through prescriptions. I wanted to help them fix the underlying issues in their daily habits to improve their health and quality of life. One day it hit me. I had to stop running from my purpose if I was truly committed to saving the lives of those around me. Teaching others to be fit, fabulous, and fulfilled without prescribed pills through intentional changes in their lifestyle is the driving force in every aspect of my life.

When I was at the lowest and weakest point in my depression, I learned some pivotal lessons about my gift. I wondered each day if that would be the day that I went through with taking my life. I barely recognized the reflection staring back at me. My eyes were puffy and red with tears. I couldn't eat, sleep, or even think. I was tired of crying, tired of hurting, and tired of living with the pain. I was so incredibly sad and hopeless that I thought that suicide was the only way to stop my pain. God had another plan! I was gifted a three-day pass to the gym by a coworker, and that changed everything for me. As I exercised, the sadness started to subside. I began eating healthier and reading about the healing properties of food and meditation. My appetite came back, and my mood stabilized. I no longer felt like I was in a fog. For the first time in a long time, things were crystal clear. I fully understood that my work as a healer far exceeded pills and liquids in prescription bottles and people in hospital beds. The prescription that I was intended to dispense to the world was the synergy that food, physical activity, and stress management have in healing you from the inside out. So, the failures of my other businesses were a blessing. They cleared the path for me to use my personal experiences and expertise to transform lives all over the world through my videos, books, and online programs.

When I finally stopped allowing my past entrepreneurial failures to block me from walking in my purpose as The Lifestyle Pharmacist®, I made up my mind to intentionally live my life differently. I was often reminded of these words by John C. Maxwell: "When you intentionally use your everyday life to bring about positive change in the lives of others, you begin to live a life that matters." For me, that meant embracing that I am more than plaques and degrees on a wall. I am more than the job tile given to me by America's corporate healthcare system and society. My past entrepreneurial failures were preparing me to live my truth, share it openly with the world, and help people transform their health and improve their quality of life through food and lifestyle changes instead of prescribed pills.

Here are three intentional ways you can live a fit, fabulous, and fulfilled life:

Make Over Your Mindset About Food

- Food is fuel, so fuel up with the good stuff. Your body performs optimally when it has high-quality fuel nourishing your cells and powering your organ systems. A consistent clean diet of whole grains, healthy fats, low-fat dairy, lean protein, and fruits and vegetables is key. Your body will thank you by looking and feeling fabulous!

- Food is medicine. The antioxidants, nutrients, and vitamins naturally found in fresh, high-quality foods help prevent the development of chronic diseases. Specific health ailments can also be improved and managed by incorporating specific foods into your daily routine. And yes, nature's medicine (a.k.a. food) has fewer side effects and problematic interactions than traditional medications.

Schedule Time for Weekly Self-Care

- Make a standing calendar appointment with yourself. Set aside time each week for a relaxing activity that is JUST FOR YOU! Translation—this activity does not include your spouse, fiancé, or significant other and *definitely* not the kids. I know it may sound harsh, but the point is to carve out some time away from everyone and everything at least once a week to keep your stress levels in check! You deserve it, plus your physical and mental health depend on it.

- Pamper yourself with a massage, manicure and pedicure, relaxing bubble bath, or a facial. If you are in the mood for something more active, go hiking or fishing or even treat yourself to a professional sporting event or live concert.

Surround Yourself with People Who Push You to Be Better

- Take an inventory of the people in your life. I'm going to keep it all the way real with you. As you embrace the changes required to live your life with intention, negative influences and sources of pain and drama have to go. It is very necessary to surround yourself with people who understand you and the path that you are on. You know, people who REALLY want you to win!

- Joining a community of like-minded individuals who encourage and inspire you to keep going is critical to your ongoing success. They get "it," and they get you. Speaking of community, you are invited to The FABSQUAD, my amazing online community of women who are taking action to make over their lifestyle and be "fit, fabulous, and fulfilled without prescribed pills."

Intentionally Living Beyond the Secret

Lisa L. Pena

GIFT:
INTENTION

Through ups and downs, trying to get it right, and sometimes just walking where the wind blows me, I have finally come to a place where I can say: "I love the life God has given me!" I have learned to live intentionally in the moment, not yearning for what is ahead. I have allowed my spirit to be present at all times, allowed God to direct my path, listened to His guidance, and been faithful and trusting of His word.

The story I am about to tell you is my story of finally reaching *intentional* living—God's way. A story that demonstrates how God can use what others intend for your harm for His goodness. Through pain and suffering, God can intentionally transform and use us to bring us to places today we might not have gone otherwise.

I am a mother of three children, founder of a Montessori school and foundation, and in general, a humanitarian who survived a 21-year abusive marriage. All and all, I am just an ordinary person trying to live each day intentionally. It is what I learned later in life that helped me become fully present, living intentionally and receiving peace, no matter my circumstances. My motto in life is: "Little by little by little can make a lot of a difference in this world."

My brother and I were raised in a household of two wonderful parents who provided a lifetime of experiences that made us healthy and happy. When I was growing up, my dad owned a struggling business. When his business eventually failed, he reverted to "Plan B," which was to return back to the education field and become an administrator for the local public school system. His return to education allowed him to provide for his family. He was well respected in his position. The failure of his business was clearly intentional in God's plan, and he would plant seeds in me that would blossom me into entrepreneurship.

My mother was a wonderful role model. She graduated from college at age 37, became the director of personnel and budget at Brown and Montgomery College, the first African American and female vice president at Princeton University, and first female vice president at Johns Hopkins University. This all happened to a woman who was raised on a poor tobacco sharecropping farm in Upper Marlboro, Maryland. I admire how my mom overcame so many obstacles. I can clearly see that her journey was intentional and all in God's plan, and I can see the seeds of perseverance she planted in me.

Born in the 60s and raised in the 70s, I grew up when everyone in the neighborhood took care of each other, parents didn't micro-manage, there were no cell phones, and everyone ate dinner together. The neighborhood was a pillar of security for all who lived there. It quickly changed from an all-Jewish neighborhood to one that housed people from all walks of life. Walking down the streets of our neighborhood was a unique experience— smelling foreign spices, hearing multiple languages spoken, seeing multiple cultures from just about anywhere around the world. Providence had become a melting pot of the world. I know my parents had many struggles during our upbringing, but my brother and I didn't feel them. We were blessed with our upbringing, experiences, and friendships. We were exposed to all walks of life, and our parents encouraged us to love, respect others, and offer our best to this world. Somewhere along the way, I lost sight of those fundamentals.

So how does this independent woman from an upbringing fostered in love and respect find herself in a marriage that consists of physical and verbal abuse? That's the million-dollar question!

Domestic violence does not have a stereotypical look. It spans through all socio-economic backgrounds and is more present than meets the eye. I first dated my ex-husband when I was 17, we became exclusive when I was

19, we got married when I was 24, and we got divorced when I was 46. From the outside, our married life looked perfect. We had three children, made six-figure incomes, and built a home in a golf course community. At the point of separation, we owned three homes and five vehicles and traveled pretty freely. It looked like perfection. Why would I want to disturb that?

I was masking a lie. Our house was miserable, and everyone in it was walking on eggshells, not knowing when the next bomb would explode. Our home was one that was full of extremes: extreme ups and extreme downs, but not a whole lot of leveling in between, when "He" was home.

It was not until near the end of my 20+ year journey living with abuse that I realized the reality of the "culture" I accepted for my family. Prior to this awareness, I considered the abuse as incidences and not a lifestyle. In an attempt to keep my family whole, I was ironically making my family broken.

I remember the day that my daughter saved my life and the life of our whole family like it was yesterday. We were on a Caribbean family vacation in a private home with another family. I remember my ex getting in my daughter's face, screaming and yelling at her, humiliating her in front of our friends, and even spitting while yelling, all because she was a vegetarian. For me, that was the breaking point that turned the light bulb on. It was at that very moment that I was finally able to see vicariously through my daughter's eyes. I could finally see what my children and I had been living through. My soul that I had protected for so many years was now confronted and had to submit to reality and walk in truth. The humiliation my daughter had to endure forced me to look at myself in the mirror and lift that veil that had been covering my reality for well over 20 years. At that point, I had no choice but to let my soul be my guide and see the light. That day, God gave me a new pair of eyes, which allowed me to recognize the abuse and acknowledge that I wanted out and gave me the courage to move. Ding! Ding! Ding! I got it! I could finally see that my sucking it up for "the better of the whole" was, in fact, harming the whole family. And though it took me eight long months after that incident to leave the home and get re-established, I made it out, and my children and I live a new life!

It took a while for me to forgive myself for the offenses I allowed my children and myself to live through. I can finally say I love my life, but not because it is one to envy or even because I feel that everyone would want to be me or go through what I went through. I know that through my experiences, I have become the woman God expected me to be. It was through my ups and downs, especially my downs, that I grew with God. When I hit rock bottom and felt like I was on an island alone trying to survive, I prayed, gained humility, acquired strength (from the Lord), and gained courage to deal with life head on. I have shown up, I am living in the now, and I love my life! Thank you, Lord! I live intentionally and can see God using my experiences to bring others closer to Him.

God gifts us His fruits of the Holy Spirit by which to live: love, joy, peace, patience, kindness, goodness, faithfulness, gentleness, and self-control. I have lived a life trying to abide by them. God wants us to use judgment, and not the type of judgment that makes us better than our neighbor, but the type of judgment that allows us to surround ourselves with good will that will make us a stronger servant for His Glory. Be aware. Many will prey on us, and we owe it to ourselves and the Lord to make sure the gifts that God has given us are always in the right hands.

Thirty-three years from my first moment of abuse by my ex, I am now dating my brother's childhood best friend, a childhood neighbor and someone I have known since I was seven years old. God has shown me, for the first time in my life, how He intends for me to be treated and brought me a man who is equally yoked. It's funny how God intentionally sent me around the world, only to return back where I originally started—back to a foundation of love and respect.

"You intended to harm me, but God intended it for good to accomplish what is now being done, the saving of many lives."
—Genesis 50:20 (NIV)

This Little Light: The Hidden Diamond Among the Ashes

Makena Gargonnu

GIFT:
INTENTION

Back in 2005, I was a social worker for almost four years for a nonprofit agency that worked with at-risk youth to provide services to assist them with job preparation, work readiness workshops, academic assessments, and coaching to be successful in school. I really enjoyed my job, but in the back of my mind, I always wondered how I would manage my special event planning business, which I loved, full-time. My caseload grew from 35 to 75 students because of previous layoffs, and I was also a single mother and trying to build a business on the side.

One day, a miracle happened while I was sitting at my desk. I got a call from a comedian named Daryl Mooney who heard about my event planning services on an LA radio show. He said I was highly recommended and wanted to see if I would partner with him and his brother Dwayne to produce wealth seminars in San Diego. I was blown away. What an opportunity! It was like God heard my prayers and put some fire on it!

From this point on, I start thinking about how I was going to do more events, but I didn't know how I was going to accomplish all of this, as I had just gotten married to the love of my life, was pregnant with my second child, and still had the demands of being a social worker to deal with. The stress was heightened even more when one day I got an unexpected call to meet with my supervisor. At this meeting, she and another co-worker decided that if I didn't have my case files updated for an audit in 30 days, I would be fired from my job. Keep in mind that as a company, our caseloads were tripled. The maximum number of cases that a social worker should be given is only 25, and I had 75. I had to figure out how to get this done in 30 days!

I believe that sometimes fiery situations in our lives occur for us to raise up out of the ashes to find out what we are truly made of. The unknown pressure that we are currently experiencing will either numb us, break us, or raise us up to the sparkling diamond that we are. I chose to rise up! I mapped out a plan every day to get caught up on all my case notes. I put in my regular 40 hours a week, picked up my 10-year-old son from school, and relentlessly worked on my case notes at night and on weekends. This pressure woke me up! I realized at this moment I was more than just a mandated reporter. I needed to be the event producer I was so strongly desiring to be.

I knew this stress was unhealthy for my new life I had just begun, and I wanted change. After tireless hours, I met the deadline, and my supervisor couldn't believe I had gotten it done. In our meeting, I shared with her that I'm an educated professional, and when you give me a task to complete, I will get it done at all costs. This time of pressure trained me to be a diamond shining brightly in the darkest situations.

Months later, God gave me my answer. All the remaining case managers were laid off because the funds from our grant were all used up. While many case managers were upset, I celebrated! I was free! I was seven months pregnant and ready to explore the possibilities of doing special event planning full-time. Thankfully, my husband supported my crazy proposal to not go back to work.

I realize now that there are five ways in which I use my former social justice work in my thriving event planning business:

Assess the situation. In the social worker world, you have to meet with people who have needs that aren't being fulfilled in their lives. Many times, my students were coming from broken homes, their parents were working long hours, and many of them didn't have positive people to look up to. I would have to meet with them one on one and check on their grades, discuss their plans for their future, and see what resources were available. In the event planning world, I have to do the same thing. I assess what I feel the client needs to combat in a world that gives them uncertainty. If they are stressed out, I produce comedy shows to make them laugh. If women are suffering from high blood pressure and making poor eating choices, I produce a spa party for them to destress. I'm always look for ways to help people create change in their situation.

Listen to clients' problems. As a social worker, I would spend 30 minutes to an hour listening to a child's situation about why something at school wasn't working for them. I wouldn't judge the story but just maintain good eye contact and try to empathize with their woes or concerns. In my business, I have to do that with my clients. I sometimes sit with them at a coffeehouse or talk to them over the phone and listen to why they want to produce an event. My goal is to understand their expectations and create a blueprint and execute a plan to make that event come to life.

Make a plan. Once I assessed my clients' situation in my social worker world, I began to plan out the best way to help them ease their way out of their situation or eliminate the problem altogether. For example, one my students' mother kicked her out when she turned 18 years old right in the beginning of the school year because she recently got married and no longer wanted her daughter in the home. As a case manager, I had to first emotionally support my client but also start thinking of teen shelters where she could stay so she wouldn't be homeless while going to school. I went beyond my job description to find a safe place for her to live. As an event producer, I have to plan an event from the beginning to the end. In other words, we think about how we want the event to look at the end and plan day by day and week by week each activity we need to do to make it happen. Where is the venue? Who is the entertainment? Who will be on the invitation list? Once we figure out the intricate details, we use our plans to make an event a success.

Find the appropriate resources and the best professionals to help. With the agency I was with, we had over 20 partners who provided resources to help our students. One partner could help with transportation for trips, another would purchase bus passes if my students were hired for a new job, and some partners even helped the students find employers. One of the most important tasks was to make sure the resources were credible. I had to make sure the company was legitimate, highly recommended, and safe for my students to receive services. In event planning, I have to find the right professionals to work on various events—those who are dependable, friendly, detailed oriented and can work under extreme pressure.

Create a win-win for all parties involved! As a case manager, I knew my main job was to make my students happy and be sure that they received all the love and attention they needed to succeed. It was about what they wanted for themselves. Our sessions together were about helping them dig up what was already inside of them so they could improve their home life, grades, friendships, and work life.

As a celebrity event producer, I work with comedians, authors, speakers and high-profile entrepreneurs who need someone with whom they can share their vision. I can immediately imagine the future of the event and make it happen. My underlining purpose is my clients' and partners' happiness and allowing their company to flourish through impactful events. For the past 12 years, I have been self-employed doing what I love from my home office, creating events in my hometown and beyond!

Dreams Become Reality Through Intention

Paula Dezzutti

My name is Paula Dezzutti Hewlette, but these days, I am better known as Pixie Paula. I spent decades in the sleepy woods of Northwestern Connecticut, but currently I pack and unpack my suitcase in Charleston, South Carolina. My education and business discipline launched me into the world as a skilled financial, tax planning, and real estate investor before fate had its way and I was thrust into an industry I didn't even know existed but now is the very passion behind my existence. What really drives me? The fact that I gave birth to nine children and became an ordained minister seems to pale in comparison to what I experienced since I entered the reality TV world. In 2009, I became a founding investor and director on the board of a cutting-edge technology company that is disruptive to the most lucrative industry on the planet—alcohol! Pixie is now the CEO of Local Choice Spirits, a family-run, award-winning brand development and distribution platform combining the strength of super premium spirits with top-notch celebrity artists and a pioneering loyalty initiative that is a game changer in brand marketing.

So, what happened next? The declaration of **intention**! I had a distinction a long time ago that helped me to understand and improve the odds of my not only getting what I wanted in my own backyard, but also finding worldwide connections over the last several years, resulting in being featured in *USA Today Magazine, The Huffington Post, INC Magazine, Yahoo Finance, Dow Jones Market Watch, Whiskey Passion Magazine, Entrepreneur Mind World*, and more. And none of this matters unless you understand *how* it happened. Was it fate? Positive thinking? The luck of the dice? I don't think so. I think the simple little secret to all of this was **INTENTION**! Some people call this the "Law of Attraction"—what you think about, you bring about. And what you think about with passion, you bring about quickly. How does intention turn into manifestation? Does it even matter?

Intention sounds like a big word because it moves big energy. A lot of people have big ideas but never seem to be doing anything about them or acting upon them. Others look like they are very busy all the time but are never really getting anywhere. Their "busyness" is constant, yet they always seem to be in the same place; no upward growth; decades of doing the same thing over and over again. The magic happens when intention is met with timely action, and then you *must* follow this model repeatedly. There is no room for stagnation; you have to put your pedal to the medal all the time! If you remain absorbed in your intention while having the focus to stay your course and keep all your valves open, you will never burn out and your intention can't help but turn into the manifestation of your heart's desires. Remember, this is not "busyness." This is not **doing**, this is **intending**.

So, if intention is what is creating the world around you, how do you monitor and ensure your results? The name of the game is to narrow the gap in time from when you self-discover an intangible desire of yours, declare it as an intention out to the universe, and then behold what actually shows up in physical form. Can you make a declaration and just *will* it into being? On great authority, we have heard about miracles: "God said, let there be light… and there was light." If we are made in the likeness and image of our Creator, what powers do we actually have? Jesus said, "And you too will do greater works than these." Ask yourself what intention others see in you. If you want to know what you're committed to in life, look at your life. Life doesn't happen to you, it happens through you. You are the only one driving the bus. Life certainly didn't fall out of the sky and land on your face. You are the creator, and you make up your story through intention. You have already mapped out your story in your head and your heart. Every little detail is in alignment with your intention or left as a disappointment from an expectation that you may not have consciously known you had. But now you're knowingly sad, and you don't even know why. It's because you have removed yourself from the connection to your truth, your self, and your intention.

You see scam artists and street hustlers pulling a racket on some unsuspecting soul to steal their goods. In a way, your own unsuspecting thoughts rob you of your success and overpower your good intentions. Why? Because there's a payoff in that for you. If you were honest, you would be able to identify what that payoff was. Does it allow you to be lazy, avoid the embarrassment of failure, eliminate the call to action, and conceal your ignorance? Or worse, does it keep you from truly becoming the dreamer you were born to be? Did you replace your inspiration with a course of action that was more controlled and rigorous and filled with rules? Do you continually deny yourself from actually reveling in the secret that we own our power—all of it? Is this illusion keeping you from being a responsible and accountable strategist with yourself whilst keeping success at bay? To move out of mediocrity, you must never, ever close your valve. Keep the juices flowing. The right answers will be rewarded to those who are asking the right questions. You know the saying, "To those whom much is given, much is required"? Was the "much is required" part simply the difficult task of intention? Can you believe in Santa Claus?

When I surrendered from belaboring in my head what I had to lose if I just tried the practice of intention,

I discovered in my heart a road of cause and effect that would forever change my course of action. I fell in love with my declarations and intentions; ultimately my life moved from the elaborate visions I was dreaming about in my head into the manifestation of physical materials I could touch, love, and drive! I began to feel so alive and magical that I could hardly discern if I was in my head or outside of my head. Soon I realized that it didn't really matter where I was or how I got there. There is really nowhere to go, nothing to do, and no one to be. It is all self-imposed. How liberating to discover that there doesn't have to be a time lag between your stated intention and how you experience your manifestation, knowing that the joy of life lies simply in your intention alone.

I am living the greatest intention of my life journey so far, and it all started as a dream. Literally a dream! You know when you wake up from a dream that is so intense that it takes a few minutes to discern if it was real or just a dream? And you can't shake off the mystical feeling you are in, so you tell everyone as if almost trying to convince yourself that it was just a dream? That's how this was for me. I will never forget it. it was January 1, 2011—you know, 1:1:11! I awoke with every step of the next part of my journey being completely laid out for me. I thought to myself, "That was some bad Chinese food I ate last night... or dreams are actually our suppressed intentions breaking through!" This was a distinction that came in with a vengeance. I had been asking the universe for answers on how to market my new products, and I had just awoken from a dream where I was actually living out the end results simply by owning my intention and declaration and appreciating the success of my actions. I ran to the computer to search for the concept of a partnership marketing platform. I called my attorney and shared my dream with her. I ran it by a few people as if it was actually already in existence. And surprisingly, everyone I told received it. They got the message! I started telling everyone, "I had a dream! I had a dream!" I know it sounds like I stole the line, but maybe the line is "given" to us! How many of us have been given the dream, given the line, and fail to stand in the power of intention? But just like every good movie that you hope has a happy ending when the protagonist steps in and the hero looks like she will be defeated by the villain, the naysayers stepped in to boisterously share their unwarranted opinions. But this time things were different for me. Negativity had already been played out in the dream. I had already dealt with the people who couldn't see my vision and was able to walk right on by them. I could appreciate their lack of vision and limited bandwidth as the reason *I* was chosen for the job. This belonged to me! What belongs to *you*?

The Power of Intention

Renay L. Butler

GIFT: INTENTION

There is something magical about living your life with intention. To be intentional is to thoroughly plan for things you want to achieve. With intention, you can craft a better plan, achieve faster results, prepare for or eliminate obstacles, and achieve the successes you've dreamed of. Magical things begin to happen when you infuse your God-given talents with intention; this is a sure-fire winning combination! God gives each of us gifts that we nurture throughout our lifetime. He places people in our paths for a reason or season to aid in manifesting our destiny.

I share my story of intention because I want each of you to know that no matter the obstacles or goals, you can conquer anything with intentional thought and planning.

It was an early Saturday morning. I sat quietly in the office of the business I'd worked to build for the past

10 years. I began reflecting on my journey because this would be the last time I sat in "this" office.

Eleven years prior, the internet start-up bubble began crashing, and I was laid off from my corporate job as an IT project manager. I remember driving home thinking, "What am I going to do?" When I arrived home, I immediately pulled out my journal. But instead of writing, I began reading entries from the last year trying to find some clarity. I found over 10 entries that referenced "children learning new technologies" or "volunteering opportunities to teach children about technology." I took a mental note but also knew I needed to be still to hear God's voice.

The next day while driving my daughter to school, I heard a voice say, "Start a daycare." I brushed it off because my training up to this point was technology, business, and sales. Later that day, I again heard a voice whisper, "Daycare." I pondered the idea but again brushed it off. As the first week went by, I busied myself with catching up on overdue house projects, early fall cleaning, de-cluttering, and donating old clothes and items. I am a firm believer that you have to get rid of the old to allow for new energy to flow, so I was preparing my mind and my home for this next phase of life.

Week two, I decided to update my resume and do a bit of searching on the internet for IT positions. During my searches, I found myself Googling "daycares." I jotted down a few ideas in case I pursued this route. I started with "teach kids about technology." I kept writing until I exhausted all of my thoughts. The next day, I received a letter in the mail from Women Entrepreneurs of Baltimore, Inc. (WEB) with an offer to compete for a scholarship to attend their business training program. I began completing the application and I got to the question, "What type of business are you interested in starting?" I wrote "Daycare," closed my eyes, and prayed. I asked God to guide me through this journey if this was what He intended for my life.

A few weeks later, I got a call to come in for the first rounds of competency testing and interviews. Within the next few weeks, I was notified that I was one of 20 people selected out of several thousand applicants to enter the program. I was elated because I knew at that moment that God was ordering my steps and that the next four mouths would be a journey filled with new beginnings and intention.

I knew that my every step would need to be well thought out. As a certified project manager, this is what I did best. After all, I'd managed multiple million-dollar-plus projects simultaneously and led award-winning teams, so surely, I could do this. I spent every waking moment, about 20 hours a day, meticulously choreographing my execution. I had class Monday, Wednesday, and Friday at WEB from 9 a.m.–5 p.m. On Tuesdays and Thursdays and every week night, I enrolled in child development coursework at the local community college and the Child Resource Center. Over the course of the next four months, I would complete over 20 training classes and earn my certification as Childcare Center Director. This was huge! This meant I could own a large facility versus an in-home center.

Women Entrepreneurs of Baltimore was my new happy place. On the first day of class, we were handed a large binder with our coursework. After introductions, our instructor said, "It is our expectation that when you complete this training, the doors of your business will be open and fully operational within one month of graduation. You are expected to attend every class and complete every assignment."

Each day, I showed up to absorb everything we were taught. I'd go home, do my research, complete my homework, and input data into my business plan. I knew this was a once-in-a-lifetime opportunity, and I had to take full advantage of it. WEB taught me every aspect of business, including developing a winning business plan, marketing, finance, fundraising, advertising, taxes, real estate negotiations, contracts, and human resources. Each week, industry leaders were brought in to teach and mentor us, but more importantly, we were connected to the people and resources we each needed to start and operate a successful business. This was better than any textbook or college class.

At each step in my journey, God put people in my path at the exact time I needed them to help move me to the next level. I was all in! I was excited, committed, and determined. I moved with intention with everything I did, including selecting the location of my daycare.

The educational programs I'd developed were infused with technology; we would also have laptops and webcams in every classroom and a computer lab. There was a high school in another county that was selected as a pilot school to integrate technology into their classrooms as well. I intentionally selected a location that would be a feeder daycare to the elementary school that fed the middle school that fed that high school. I wanted "my" kids to be ahead of the curve and well prepared for the emerging world of technology.

A few weeks before graduation, my business plan was complete. I'd found a location, applied for a business loan with the Small Business Administration (SBA), received my Center Director's certification, and had a ton of classes under my belt. I was ready, and I was exhausted. I couldn't remember the last time I'd slept more than four hours. I was lying in my bed, and the phone rang. It was one of the women we'd met from the local newspaper inviting me to a networking event about an hour away. Did I say I was exhausted? I declined, and she said, "Renay, you really should come, it's a great opportunity to network." I dragged myself out of bed, got dressed, and attended the event.

I worked the room, introduced myself to almost everyone there, and exchanged business cards and pleasantries, but I was ready to go. I was standing next to a gentleman having idle chit-chat when he asked what I did. I excitedly told him about my new business venture. He was so impressed and shared in my excitement. He then said, "I'm the final signature on all SBA loans in the state. I'll pull your application tomorrow and make sure it gets approved." I thanked him immensely, as I was told it may take months for approval. My loan was approved the next day, and I signed the lease to my 10,000-square-foot daycare facility.

We opened the doors a few months later, and that is where I poured my heart and soul for the next nine years until I was presented an offer to sell that I couldn't refuse. It was a bittersweet moment; I smiled as I handed over the keys to my empire knowing God would soon order my next steps.

This journey taught me so many lessons of faith and determination, but more importantly, I gained the tools and knowledge I would need for my next journey. I have gone on to become a business consultant and have helped hundreds of others start or grow their own businesses. I am blessed with the gifts of invention, creation, and business. My project management training gives me the ability to take big-picture ideas and break them into manageable parts, therefore allowing me to seamlessly help others create successful "idea-to-product" paths.

I leave you with these final words: "Your vision is your destiny." Pray about your journey, envision yourself in it, write it all down, and be fearlessly intentional about achieving your goals. There is no Google map for your life, so listen to your heart and God's whispers to chart a path that allows you to use your gifts and talents to make this world a better place.

Forgiveness

I Can't Take It Anymore

Curtis Venters

GIFT:
FORGIVENESS

I can't take it anymore, living my life in pain and sorrow. I can't take it anymore, not bringing the light to the darkness. I can't take it anymore, sitting on the sidelines and not being an active participant in making change. I can't take it anymore, not being the change that I want to see. I can't take it anymore, not being the one you can depend on. I can't take it anymore, not being great or living in my greatness.

I looked out the window into the cloudless sky and thought, what else could possibly happen? There was so much on my plate; I just didn't know how much more I could take.

My son had called me earlier that day and asked me for some money. I love my children with all my being, so of course I gave him what he needed. What no one knew is that I was on my way to take that very money to pay my water bill. At that moment, I was broke, busted, and tired. I had been working 12- to 16-hour days at the salon to drown the pain of my mother's death.

When I wasn't working and the pain hit me, I would resort to substance abuse. So this particular day, I got high as a kite and said, "To hell with all this. I can't take no more! What else?" My high, my sorrows, and I went straight to my mothers' grave.

I lay on that grave and I cried and cried! I tried to cry, drug, and work my life away. I decided that I didn't want to live anymore. This had to end. I was going to take my life. I couldn't take it anymore.

As I sat at the grave contemplating what method I would use to take my life, I envisioned my sisters, my father, and my mother. Moreover, I began to visualize my children and the pain on their faces from losing me. God forbid they go through this pain unnecessarily, all because I couldn't take it anymore. I had to make it through! I had to do this!

So, I got myself up from that grave, and I told myself to press on. I pressed my way home. Pressed my way through that front door straight to the bathroom to relieve myself only to discover my water had been turned off! I couldn't even flush the dang toilet! Can you believe this?

Instead of asking what else could happen, I took my little, high, depressed tail outside, got a trash can, and filled it with water. I dragged it back to my house and used the water to flush my toilet. I was beginning to learn to keep going beyond my feelings. I refused to sit in depression and smell crap too! I had to be the change that I wanted to see.

There is an emotional state of numbness when you go through a series of unfamiliar situations. One of those situations is death. There is nothing to prepare us for the sting of losing a loved one, especially when it is the loss of a parent.

I was my mother's firstborn and her only son. Oftentimes, my family would mention that I was her favorite. My mother loved us all the same, but we did have our own special relationship. She cherished me, and I cherished her. You don't know how to act when your loss takes a chunk of your heart. You don't know how to respond to the pain. You just have to move through the experience.

One thing I learned through my mother's passing was how to transition with dignity. You see, my mother lived with grace and dignity, and she transitioned with that same grace and dignity. My mother believed that anything I wanted to do in this life, I could. She always believed in me and taught me it wasn't what you did, but how you did it. She was my biggest cheerleader, the family matriarch, and the glue holding everything together.

My mother believed that being prepared was the key to any successful endeavor, and she was correct. Preparation is everything. When opportunity meets preparation, success is inevitable. Before passing, my mother encouraged me through my divorce. She instilled these values in all her children—my three sisters and me. Now, I had to go through it alone.

My father instilled in us a work ethic; he taught us hard work, determination, and tenacity and reminded us to never give up—a quitter never wins, and a winner never quits. The teachings of my mother and my father were the two forces that got me through what seemed to have been the worst time of my life. Although these times were challenging and difficult to bare, they were experiences that shaped my life.

None of us are going to evade these situations unless we are the subjects of the situation, no matter how hard we try. We don't always get to control the outcome, but if we embrace the situation, we can learn to overcome it successfully.

I have learned not to ask, "What else?" Oh no, Buddy! So, I learned. I learned to look at what I could take away from the current situation. I learned to realize that if you're looking up and there are clouds, then you continue to walk and you will see a break in those clouds through which there is light. I learned that if you're looking down on darkness, then darkness is what you will see. Not only will you see the darkness, but it will begin to magnify itself.

However, when you recognize the darkness and make a purposed decision to focus on the light, that darkness will shrink and be overtaken by the light. At that moment, you will no longer walk in the darkness because you have chosen to live in the light. It is a hard thing for us to comprehend light over dark, especially when we are in the darkest times of our lives.

You could be like me and feel that in the midst of darkness, being overworked and high is light. But my friend, that is just more darkness. What feels like disparity at its highest height is only strength building. You can get through this, and you will get through this.

Sitting down and doing nothing is the worst thing any person can possibly do. You can either choose to sit and wallow in sorrow, or you can get up and choose to live a life greater than yourself. Look outside of your hurt, pain, and issues and open your eyes to your neighbor.

That person next to you may be going through the very thing you are or at least something similar. You may even open their eyes to the realization that what they are going through isn't that bad. Focus your energy on serving. Once you change your focus, you will start to notice your life changing.

Once I received that revelation, I thought more about others and less about me. I began to reach out to others who were in states of desperation, despair, and depression and experiencing similar situations, not to minimize what they were going through or to set myself up as some type of counselor or know-it-all in their life, but to let them know that they were not alone. To let them know I empathize with them because I've been there. I can empathize because I know exactly what it feels like to lose a great treasure.

Also, I want to encourage others because I know what it feels like to be discouraged. The feelings of loss never go away, but there is goodness in the loss. Although this had to happen, it happened for a reason. You may think what I just said is a cliché, but everything *does* happen for a reason—not just one reason, but many reasons, and not just for you, but also for those around you and the stranger down the street.

One of the hardest things I found to do is to get up after a fall. Anybody can smile when things are going well, but it takes a person of serious faith to smile through challenging times. It's not because you think your situation is funny or you are crazy and delirious and not taking things seriously. It's because you are taking things seriously.

You seriously know that things will be okay. Seriously, I am not going to stay here in a broken place. Seriously, I have come out of trying situations before, and I will do the same now. Sometimes you don't know exactly when you're going to come out of it, but you know for a fact that you will, just as you have all the other times. That alone is encouraging. Just remember to be the change that you want to see in the world.

In a Whisper

Heidi Lewis

GIFT:
FORGIVENESS

Mommy, are you okay?

In a whisper "Don't worry I'm okay, I'll fix it."

Running to her aide. Wanting to fight with her, to be
by her side like soldiers

as she escaped the center of the rifle against her chest.

Her strength was hidden in a whisper.

—Monique Lewis

He lied, and I'm angry! Why can't he just tell the truth?
Everyone knew he beat my mother. Half listening as my
sister recounts the conversation, I visualize an incident
that occurred when we were children. I was shocked at
how vividly I could remember it—colors and sounds and
smells. I could see the blood stain the front of my mom's
peach-colored blouse, the sound of our screaming, and
the look on her face as she tried to hide her fear. I can

still remember the look of contempt and satisfaction on his face as if he'd accomplished some great feat. I shudder now because all of the old feelings that I thought were behind me come rushing to the forefront. The old hate and rage fill my entire being. I can taste the bile in my mouth. Trying to shake them off, I turned my attention back to the conversation with my sister.

"Heidi, I don't understand why he treated Mom that way."

"I don't know. Girl, it's late, and I have to get up early," I say to my sister as I hang up the phone.

He isn't our biological father. Our dad passed away when we were very young. He seemed to come along when we needed someone to fill the void left by our dad's passing. He taught us to fish and took us camping. He protected us from the neighborhood bullies and was the first man to tell me I was pretty. When did the abuse begin? Perhaps it was always there and was kept hidden from us. When did he become the abusive alcoholic monster who terrorized us and caused us to live in fear? I have no answers to the questions that invade my mind. All I know is, he's a liar. I'm an adult now who isn't afraid of him anymore. "I'm not afraid," I think as I lie awake with tears in my eyes. I begin to pray, "God, help me."

As a little girl, I used to watch my mom comb her hair and apply her makeup. She would show me how to put on eyeliner and lipstick and tell me what colors would go with my complexion. This was always my favorite time with her. To me, she was beautiful. All I wanted to do was make her proud. Then one day, as I followed her into the bathroom, she told me no. I didn't understand, so I pushed the door open and saw the bruises on her body. I watched her take little red pills (I learned much later that the pills were Valium). The look in her eyes stopped me from asking her if she was okay. I think there was a knowing. I finally understood the bumps in the night, the silent cries, the distraught look on her face, and why she spoke in a whisper. That moment felt like a lifetime. She finally told me to close the door and go to my room.

The bumps in the night became louder and more frequent until they became full-fledged beatings that took place in front of us and others. By the time I was 14 years of age, I decided that I'd had enough and that I was going to defend my mother at any cost. He slapped her one night in front of a house full of guests. I hurried into the kitchen and pulled a knife out of the butcher block. Running back into the living room, I lunged at him, screaming, "If you touch my mother again, I will kill you!" This heart-stopping rage felt as if I were having an out-of-body experience. It took my uncle and two other men to get the knife away from me.

After that, he would taunt me, "The next time you pull a knife on me, you better use it, otherwise I'll break your neck." I was afraid, but I used his words against him. He had taught us to never let "them" see you sweat. So, I would stand up to him. I was determined not to allow him to treat me like he did my mother.

The last straw for my mom came when I was 19. He punched a hole in the wall and threatened to kill my sister. I will never forget sitting at the dining room table all night with my mother as she held a knife in her hand, promising to take him out if he touched my sister.

"No one is ever going to beat my ass again or touch my children," she said in a low growl.

The next morning, she told him to leave. Just like that, he was gone out of our lives. The trauma remained. We crouched past the windows of our apartment afraid he may be outside with the rifle. We walked to the bus stop in pairs and looked around every corner.

So, as I lay awake with the memories swirling around in my mind, I decided to confront him. His lies were too much for me to handle. It was time for him to own his stuff. I was going to see to it. I rehearsed what I was going to say and do. I was going to ask him why he beat my mother and then wait for him to lie so that I could cite dates and times. I was going to remind him of the Christmas that he pushed her to the floor, the time he threatened her life if she attended my fashion show or the day she stabbed him in the face with her nail file to stop him from beating her. I disregarded the fact that I'd asked God to help me. The more I continued plotting his demise, the more God was gently convicting my heart. I knew it, but I was determined to hurt my stepfather the way he had hurt us, the way he had hurt my mom. I knew I wasn't okay with God.

A few days later, I was speaking with a friend, sharing my situation and what I planned to do. She said to me, "Heidi, forgiveness isn't for the other person, it's for you. What happens when you confront your stepdad and he doesn't apologize? You have to be okay with that." She told me that bitterness was in my heart. I hadn't considered that forgiveness wasn't about letting my stepdad off the hook, but about allowing myself to move forward.

I thought I knew what the Bible says about forgiveness, but during the conversation with my friend and the encounter with my memories, I knew that I didn't. I realized that if I didn't forgive, how could I expect God to forgive me? I began to search the scriptures to see what they said about forgiveness and bitterness. Here's what I found:

"Who is a God like you, who pardons sin and forgives the transgression… You don't stay angry forever but delight to show mercy" (Micah 7:18-19, NIV). This verse changed my life. It taught me that if God didn't stay angry with me and showed me mercy, I needed His help to show the same mercy to my stepfather. Secondly, I realized that the way I responded when I felt as if I were being "punked" was based on my childhood. Anger would spring up from the pit of my stomach, and it impacted everyone around me. Again, I used the Bible as a reference; "See to it that no one comes short of the grace of God; that no root of bitterness springing up causes trouble, and by it many be defiled" (Hebrews 12:15, NASB). I learned that I wasn't responsible for what happened in my childhood nor the actions of my stepfather. I am responsible for my actions. I decided that I could no longer live the life of a victim.

Am I telling you that this was an overnight process? Absolutely not. The rage and bitterness were deep within me. However, once I made the decision to be healed, I found an inner strength I didn't know was there. I heard Viola Davis say, "It may take a long time to not be broken." The little girl who was afraid to sleep at night because of the bumps in the night is still within me. But instead of being immobilized, I use her strength to propel me forward, step into my truth that I am a survivor, and forgive my past. Do I still want to hear him apologize? Sure, I do. But, I'm okay with never receiving an apology.

Letting Them Off the Hook

Angela Eugene

GIFT:
FORGIVENESS

According to the prophet Jeremiah in the book of Jeremiah 29:11, "I believe God has a plan for your life to give you a hope and a future not to harm you."

I learned at an early age that it was taboo to share family business with anyone. Who would have thought I'm the total opposite today? I'm an open book because of my trials and tribulations. Have you ever felt like if you had done something differently, it would have changed your entire situation? Can I be honest with you? For many years, I lived with shame and anger in my heart because I thought, "How could this happen to me?" Sit back and fasten your seatbelt. Let me be transparent and share my story.

When I was 11 years old, I could not find my voice to speak up about me being molested by a close family member. There were so many emotions going on in my mind and my head. How could this happen to a sweet, innocent girl like me? My parents divorced when I was a baby, and all I could think about was that I could not tell my mom. At the time, all I saw in my mind was a woman trying to make ends meet to ensure she had the best for her child. The last thing she needed to hear was someone had violated her only child. During the critical years between the ages of 12 and 14, I felt as though something was wrong with me. I was an introvert and just bottled up all my emotions on the inside. On top of all of these emotions, I was longing for that close relationship with my father, who was not present in my life. At that point in my life, I tried seeking attention from boys trying to fill a void that I realized later in life only God could fill. I remember falling on my knees in the bathroom one afternoon and praying for a father. The Lord answered my prayer by sending me a wonderful exemplary stepfather who was there for me in my critical teenage years and beyond. The following questions still ran through my mind often: Where was my father when I really needed to talk about the slick things these boys were telling me? Where was my father when I cried myself to sleep? I thought to myself, "I know he loves me, however his actions sure aren't showing me anything."

Fast forward to 1992. I got married at the age of 23. Most brides would love to have their father walk them down the aisle, wouldn't you agree? Not me. I knew I had allowed anger to grow over the years. I felt as though my stepfather had been there for me and he deserved to give me away. I remember the conversation I had on the phone with my aunt. She said, "You really should reconsider your decision." Her words went in one ear and out the other. As a resolve, my wedding planner included my father to at least stand from his seat and give me away verbally. At this point, I was just happy to be married. As I entered into my marriage, I still carried the pain of the little girl who longed for her father's love.

Can I tell you if you don't release unforgiveness, it will spill over into other areas of your life? There were high expectations I had of my husband, and on a number of occasions, I held him on the same hook on which I had my father because I now suffered with fear of abandonment. When we hit our seventh year of marriage, we had to endure a situation where trust was broken. My husband had to go away to school for a few months, so this left us with unresolved issues. There goes the abandonment issue I've been talking about. How could one resolve anything being miles apart? I began to become more angry, bitter, and unforgiving to everyone, even God. How could this happen to me? Why me, Lord? I really felt something was wrong with me. I thought getting married would help me to live happily ever after. Little did I know that marriage would be work, and it was even more work when I had a little girl inside of me who needed to be dealt with from a spiritual and professional place.

A year later, after much prayer, I sought God because I came to the end of myself and I realized I could not carry these burdens alone. I joined a local church that impacted my life by teaching me how to deal with relationships from a spiritual perspective. The little girl inside of me was now awakening because she was beginning to find her voice. How did she find her voice? I'm glad you asked. Let me tell you. The pastor of this church encouraged us to read a lot of spiritual books and to seek professional counseling. Again, in my culture, it was somewhat taboo to seek professional counseling. I followed his instructions because I knew I had to deal with these unresolved issues and let everyone off the hook. Now this was not an easy process at all. There were many occasions when I had to deal with the emotional hurt from those who had wronged me. It took everything in me to be the bigger person and put things behind me. For example, there were times when I would reach out to my father and he would tell me he was taking his son, whom he was now raising, to swimming lessons. The conversation was always about what he was doing with his son. I even recall the time I wanted my father to show up to see my son in a popular play. I was so proud, and I felt this would be a great opportunity for him to see the talent my son had. He declined the offer because he could not make it. Even as a grown, married woman, I felt rejected and unloved. What about the time I blew up emotionally at my husband because I felt he was working too many hours at his new business, giving me and the family very little time? I had to turn to prayer.

It was a cold, winter day, and I remember researching counselors. I wanted more than a professional counselor.

I asked the Lord to lead me to a professional counselor who had a spiritual background. After several sessions with my counselor, the healing began. You see, I learned to be open and transparent and express exactly what I was feeling. There was no more little girl with no voice hiding. I was able to write my father a letter and let him off the hook. I remember letting myself and my husband off the hook. I finally realized that all I went through had a purpose to help others. I could now say, "Why not you, Angie?" I know you're saying, "Okay, this sounds easy, but I can't do this. You don't know what I've been through. I'm not letting this person who wronged me off the hook."

Let me tell you why it's important to let the other person off the hook. The reality is that person has gone on with their life and oftentimes has no idea of the emotional turmoil you are experiencing. Forgiveness is not for the other person. It's for you to be free from the bondage of the hurt you have experienced. What helped me was turning the mirror on myself and asking, "Do you remember how much God has forgiven you?" Look at all of the things you did to wrong people. You asked Him for forgiveness. He threw it into the sea of forgetfulness to never bring it up again. You fall short every day, and yet He still forgives you. To paraphrase, Paul the Apostle states in Ephesians 4:32, "God has forgiven me of so much, so I no longer wanted to live a life of bitterness." I needed to live a life of love and joy. Before completing this chapter, I reached out to my father again to let him know how I truly felt over the years, and that I wanted to encourage others not to go through years of being angry and filled with bitterness and instead to let them off the hook by sharing my story. What a wonderful breakthrough for him and me. Today, our relationship has forever changed. It may not look like what I want it to look like, however I can now express love without feeling angry and bitter.

Forgiveness Is K.E.Y.

L. Tomay Douglas, MSW, CASACT

GIFT:
FORGIVENESS

Forgiveness is KEY to opening your gifts. It is something that is difficult but absolutely doable. It is Kingdom-minded, Empowering, and Yielding.

In my experience, it was understanding the purpose of forgiveness that gave me full access to my gifts. I had been betrayed in my marriage, in my family, and even in the church. I was harmed in the places that were considered most sacred. My guards were down because I did not see a reason to fear. I expected to be safe. However, the hurt that I experienced in these sacred institutions sent me into a downward spiral. The injury that I sustained was mostly emotional, psychological, spiritual, and to some extent, physical. Each injury caused me to retreat and go into hiding. Although I was mostly ostracized when I attempted to speak out, the silence and disdain from those assigned to protect, nurture, and shepherd me felt like a secondary attack. It was just as harmful to me considering what I had already endured.

While hate was a hard place for me to live, it was a place that I visited as I thought of all that was done to me. What I didn't count on was how my life would ultimately be impacted by the events that occurred. I made every effort to forgive, but there was something that fought me from it. I was always taught to forgive in the church and growing up in my family, but I couldn't recall anyone teaching the importance of saying "I'm sorry" when someone wronged you. I was angry as I watched people who harmed me move forward in their lives like nothing happened. Some even received the support of their peers and family. I was left alone.

I was alone with the insults of their stares and their misinterpretation of the truth. Sometimes I imagined what life would be like if I was no longer living. I tried hard to move past those incidents, and as I continued in other areas of my life, I was easily triggered. I wasn't happy with who I was becoming because it felt more like an unbecoming. The truth is everything I needed to succeed was already present. Everything good for me was already lined up waiting for me to retrieve it, but something was holding me back.

Unforgiveness kept me from walking through doors designed to bless me. Let me explain. Unforgiveness kept me locked up in a mental prison that affected my mind. My thought process was off. I often entertained stinking thinking, and that thinking altered my perception, which directed my course of action. You see, because I was hurt in those unlikely places or sacred institutions, I refused to get close to new people. In my mind, I thought that they would end up hurting me again, and so I found myself returning to a familiar place. I ended up returning to an ex-boyfriend. He was safe, and he wasn't the one who hurt me. However, he wasn't in a place where he could encourage me. He was just a safe person (so I thought) who wouldn't hurt me, but I couldn't see because my eyes were blinded with unforgiveness. It kept me bound to the harm I received and the effects of it. The very thing that I wanted to move away from, I actually kept close because I really didn't forgive.

Being unable to see what was in front of me was due to unforgiveness. I couldn't see what was good because I was running from the bad that happened to me. I mistakenly believed that no longer speaking to persons would help. Moreover, harboring unforgiveness caused me to miss the deceit that was currently taking place in my life. Here's the thing—I was operating in my gifts. I was running a program for teenage girls and going to school to get my first degree, but my gifts weren't opened. I was even functioning as a leader in the church I was attending at the time, but my gifts were not opened. They weren't open because they were locked up by unforgiveness. All the events that I had endured made me feel like I couldn't trust others, therefore, I had to withhold parts of me—my gifts—from them. Unforgiveness placed me in a self-imposed prison bound by chains. I could only go so far and only reach so many because of self-containment. I wasn't showing up fully and giving myself to those I served, and I definitely didn't fully engage to reach those waiting to hear my message. I was operating from a place of pain that not only made me feel powerless, but also impacted the way I interacted with others. I felt like a fraud. It was part of the unbecoming because I was born authentic. The only way I was to overcome the hardships that I faced was to recognize that forgiveness was key.

What I did not anticipate was the deep hurt I would face with the ex-boyfriend with whom I was familiar and felt safe. At an intimate family function, he announced that he wanted to marry me and wanted my mom's blessing. I was happy. I was the talk of the family, and this time, in a good way. He started coming to church with me and became very friendly with my then pastor. He told them he was marrying me. But then the unthinkable happened. He began disclosing things about my past to my former pastor and told him he really didn't want to marry me. He told my former pastor before he told me. I was humiliated. I was hurt. I was angry. I cried, and then I prayed. I asked God why, especially when I was understanding forgiveness to be the key to unlock me. God let me know that forgiveness was indeed the key, and I needed it to unlock me from what I could not see. God was showing me signs all along that something was wrong, and I refused to look outside of what was comfortable for me. In great expectation, I chose to leave the place of comfortability.

So, why is forgiveness KEY? KEY is an acronym that will help me to expound.

Forgiveness is KEY because it is **K**ingdom-minded. God gave us the gift of eternal life. He gave His only son to live out this very word for us. Jesus was rejected, called crazy, denied, betrayed, dismissed, spat on, abused, and killed for our sake. He can identify with being harmed by family. His disciples were his family as He declared, "Who is my family, but those that do the will of my father in heaven." Jesus was denied by Peter, abandoned by His followers, and betrayed by Judas. He understood being injured by those in the church because it was His own—the Jews, Pharisees, and High Priests—who conspired to have Jesus crucified. Although Jesus wasn't married, He did have a covenant (which marriage is) with his Father, and Jesus cried out to Him, "Father, why have thou forsaken me?" However, we can see one action He took as an example for us and instructions to follow. Jesus said, "Father, forgive them, for they do not know what they do." We even saw how Jesus displayed forgiveness in His conversation with the two thieves hanging on either side of Him. When Jesus was hanging on the cross, He told the one thief who accepted responsibility for his crime and was apologetic that he would be with Him in paradise. Wow, forgiveness was the key that gave life to the thief on the cross. The one who did wrong opened his gift to life, and Jesus, who did no wrong, opened gifts for us by offering Himself for us. This is why we get full access to all the gifts to which we are joint-heirs in Christ Jesus.

Forgiveness is **E**mpowering because it gives the individual doing the forgiving or seeking forgiveness the ability to discover their personal power. I understood that Jesus came that we might have life more abundantly, and I wanted to be in alignment with the mission of Christ. It was through my experience that I gained wisdom to apply and practice; I was humanized. Throughout my years of suffering, even in some of those old experiences, being empowered changed my perspective. Those situations that I faced presented me with the choice to forgive. They helped me to see that nothing was broken inside of me, and all that needed to be restored was my ability to see and forgive. I embraced the truth that forgiving others didn't make me weak. Rather, I was empowered beyond the things that I went through. Forgiveness is not giving away your power. No, it is standing in yours and partnering with God in His. Forgiving gave me the chance to release the power I let those who hurt me have over me. I was empowered to give them their stuff and not hold onto it because it didn't serve me, God, or the world.

Moving forward, I found out why forgiveness is **Y**ielding. Some may think yielding is weak. Yielding is resting in your power. It's knowing your place, worth, and impact. Yielding is operating in humility. Think of it this way. You're driving down a road, and the lane you're in has a yield sign. You slow down, sit still for a moment, and give the right of way. When you yield, you let the commuters go, the cars go. When you yield, you let things go. You let the hurt go, and you let the disappointment go. It's time for us to do that and to get to forgiveness. You have to yield and then ease back in. Once you move again, you can be confident and soar. You rest in a state of letting things that aren't good for you go. So, I came to a place where I paused, let the betrayal go, let the offenders go, and submitted to God all the lies attached to the harms, such as, "I deserved it" or "I am not worthy of love."

I yielded the reins that kept me connected spiritually and subconsciously to the offenders, torment, and painful memories to God, and I let go. In yielding, I was able to produce more because my gifts had been opened.

Looking to the word forgiveness, I can show you how it aligns with why it is KEY (**K**ingdom-minded, **E**mpowering, and **Y**ielding). I realized some additional truths from God's Word, which says, "What know you not that your body is the temple of the Holy Ghost which is in you, which you have of God, and you are not your own?" (1 Corinthians 6:19, KJV) The word also reminds us that we are to be living epistles to be read of all men. I had to keep in mind that Jesus came for the Jews first with his message, and then the Gentiles were grafted in or included. So, the message out of FORgiveness is that FORgiveness is FOR me first. In forgiving, I became free from the torment of my past hurts. It was for me, and it enabled me to come out of hiding. I decided to no longer hide my pain behind a smile or retreat in shades of greatness. It has now become my purposeful intention to let God's glory be fully manifested in my life. I also learned that secondly, forgiveness is FOR the person who committed that harmful act. Once released from me, they are now required to stand before God on their own. The choice is to own up to what they did, see the harm caused, and take responsibility for what they did. If they do, they too will have the opportunity to be grafted in and included in God's grace. By grace are we saved, not by works, lest any man boast. This makes forgiveness Kingdom-minded because I know that as I go about God's business, I am His walking temple and a living epistle in the world. Therefore, I choose to reflect God's truth as much as possible and wonderfully reflect His message of love, grace, and forgiveness to others.

In looking to the word GIVE in forGIVEness, my eyes were opened to how it is Empowering. Giving altogether is empowering. When I was operating in unforgiveness, I was unable to fully open my gifts and give them to the world because I was in a prison I made and still holding onto the reins. The reins I held onto was the power the offender had over me from the harm done, and it blocked my vision from seeing what was presently hurting me. It's why it's key. I had to GIVE back the reins and give myself the opportunity to receive all the blessings God has for me because there was a place for them. I was no longer occupied by visitations from hate and recurring memories of the offense. I became empowered when I gave over control to God. I gave myself room to grow and show up like never before.

Lastly, the NESS of forgiveNESS is a root word meaning "a state of," and it's conducive to forgiveness. Why? It's simple. Forgiveness is KEY to opening our gifts because we are called to yield to a state of remembering you first, loving your neighbor as you love yourself, and partaking in the first fruits. So, remember that forgiveness is for you first as you seek to be Kingdom-minded, Empowering, and Yielding.

Living in Unforgiveness

Patricia Gibson

"For I know the plans, I have for you..."
—Jeremiah 29:11 (NIV)

I am excited, blessed, and humbled to share this movement in tapping into your G.I.F.T.S. with you. The most powerful way to be successful is to find peace with life's events. My parents were born and raised in Kenya and came to America to take advantage of the opportunities available. My mother is a teacher dedicated to serving at our home church. My father was a social worker who enjoyed living life and helped many people with the opportunity to develop successful lives. I was born and raised in New Jersey and had the great liberty of witnessing my parents grow from living in a two-bedroom rental unit to owning their first home and raising eight children. Who would have thought the foundation they laid would lead me to be a successful realtor?

In August of 2002, I stepped onto campus and began my freshman year of college. My father didn't quite give me an option in deciding what my major would be. I was disturbed that he wasn't allowing me to make my own first MAJOR choice as an adult. The only option he gave me was the class with which I wanted to start for my accounting degree. Desiring to be a strong young black woman gave me the mindset to make decisions that I later would regret. At that time, my father had a plan for my life; but, the only plan I had was to graduate and have a successful career, whatever that looked like. I also knew that I didn't want to go back to my parents' house after I graduated because I didn't want to be "controlled" by my dad. Little did I know that the plan my dad had for me was a part of God's plan.

Three weeks later, I became homesick and wanted to be around family. After my dad declined to buy my bus ticket home until the holidays, I called my brother, and he bought my ticket to spend the weekend with him and my aunt. After arriving in the Washington, D.C. area, I woke up on a Saturday morning, and my brother came to my aunt's home to tell me I did not have a father anymore. I thought my dad found out that I left school for the weekend and decided to disown me, but he really meant our dad had passed away. I burst into tears until I fell back asleep, and woke up thinking I had a nightmare until my aunt confirmed it was my reality. Unsure of where my future was headed, I began to live my life in unforgiveness.

After my family received this devastating news, I watched my mother get up every day and take care of what needed to be done to ensure we still had a roof over our heads, food to eat, clothes on our backs, and funds to continue our education. I felt that my family had just lost our security, and our lives were about to change drastically. My mother made a choice to find ways to guarantee that her children would grow successfully regardless of our circumstances. She never had an excuse for why she couldn't do something for us. She just figured out ways to make things happen. While asking God, "Why us?" I began going through a series of emotions. I was hurt for not being able to see or speak to our dad before God took him. I kept replaying in my mind moments where I saw I could have been a better daughter. I wondered if my siblings and I would have to live life fighting the negative reputation of fatherless African American children. I was fearful of how my family was going to be protected. I became frustrated when my semester didn't end the way I wanted because I had to take a leave of absence for a funeral and was now unable to focus. I resented God because I felt it was not fair to my family to lose my dad so soon. I felt that God had robbed my family and me of the right to continue enjoying him as a father growing up and my mother the right to continue to enjoy him as a husband raising us. I decided I didn't want to go to church anymore. I didn't want to read the Bible. I didn't want to get married because my wedding wouldn't be perfect without my father walking me down the aisle. I didn't want kids because they would not have a grandfather to spoil them. If I had a successful career, my life would be just that. I would be a successful black woman with no husband or kids. I was angry! I didn't want to be bothered by anyone. I decided to stop dreaming and spent the rest of the year in my dorm wishing I could go to sleep and never wake up. I was slipping into depression. I would call my dad's cell phone several times just to hear his voice, and when I heard the beep for the voicemail, it sounded like the last beep before someone flatlined.

In the spring of 2003, I started to disassociate myself from the new friends I was making, and they would not let that happen. In my mind, they wouldn't leave me alone. But, really, they were trying to encourage me to keep living. One of my girlfriends was in marching band. She told the directors she knew a flute player and found her way to convince me to join the band. I didn't recognize then that God had revised His plan in His will for me. As I continued through college, I continued to meet people who created memorable experiences. I appreciated every moment they brought a smile to my face. In 2009, I graduated from college, got married, moved across the country with my husband, and still felt empty inside.

As my husband and I began our marriage journey, we encountered countless cycles of unhappiness. I began to feel uncertain about my marriage. As the market had crashed, employment became difficult, and I felt uncertain about my financial future. As we relocated with the military, I realized I constantly had drama and wanted out of this lifestyle. I constantly felt attacked by my so-called friends, including my husband, and started to collect grudges against them. I had countless therapy sessions in which I vented my problems and used all the excuses in the world, not experiencing solutions. This cycle kept going and going until I made the decision to check myself. I had realized that I was not being attacked by people, I was being attacked by spirits. Making the decision to turn away from God made me vulnerable to self-destruction.

When I decided to turn back to God, I was exhausted from being miserable, bitter, scared, unsure, insecure, angry, depressed, and most importantly, broke! I was desperate for peace of mind in my life and in my home, healing, happiness, a clear understanding of my future, and most importantly, closure! I learned that the choice I had made to hold grudges was draining me. I had no room in my heart for love. I acknowledged that I had checked out of life and was just a pretty walking zombie.

In making the decision not to live this cycle of life I had created for myself, I was on the hunt to learn specific steps to get out of where I was mentally, spiritually, emotionally, physically, and financially. God knew the desires of my heart, and now that I had forgiven Him, I began to see the purpose of the people He placed in my life to help me get back on track with His plan. I started not only to see His plan, but to also understand His plan.

Upon this vision, I became intentional about my purpose. I had to learn how to forgive. Learning to forgive allowed me to:

- Not be a statistic of my circumstance
- Be out of my head and allow peace for clarity
- Not make excuses
- Seek God for results

Acknowledge that I am blessed to be a blessing Even though I lost sight of God's plan, my detour still led me to my destiny. I started to walk by faith and not by fear. I thank God continuously every step of the way, even if the steps are small. I celebrate small victories in my life. My marriage became healthier, and my circle of influence secured a healthy state of mind through empowerment. While holding grudges caused my breakdowns, forgiveness delivered my breakthrough. I saw I had work to do and started my homework on forgiveness. My assignment included:

- Being **G**rateful daily for everything
- Being **I**ntentional about wanting my breakthrough
- Understanding what it means to **F**orgive
- Celebrating my **T**riumphs, whether big or small
- Defining and practicing **S**elf-love

Living in unforgiveness delayed my success. Without forgiveness, there are no G.I.F.T.S. As I returned to church, I learned that God had rewritten His will for me and that my journey was to give hope and a future.

Gaining My Power Back

Sunshine King

GIFT:
FORGIVENESS

Life can really throw a curveball when it comes to re-lationships. Some relationships can take you on a crazy rollercoaster ride. I too experienced that in my day. In the late summer of 1996, I met a guy who later became my husband and the father of our child in 2001. Sure, we had our ups and downs, but it wasn't out of control. Unfortunately, I'd noticed him increasingly crossing the line verbally. When we were dating in 1996, I informed him that I would not stay in a relationship if there was name calling or hitting and reminded him again when I noticed his gradual increase in verbal insults. I thought his behavior was due to his being between jobs. In September 2004, he pushed me into the computer in front of our son. I then grabbed our son and ran into the restroom for safety. My husband banged on the door a few times saying he was sorry, then he left the apartment.

My son and I stayed in silence for a couple of days after. On the third day, I took him to work in my car, went back home, packed my son's and my things, and moved out with the help of my mother. We then put everything in storage, and my son and I stayed with her. Suddenly, the storm started to brew. My husband began harassing me with phone calls on my cellphone and at my state job. This went on from September to November, when I had to put a protective order on him. However, things started to calm down to the point where we finally had the conversation to end our marriage and start the separation process.

On November 5, 2004, we agreed to meet with a pastor at the church around 7 p.m. to help put closure to our marriage. This would assist us in starting the process of our separation with the agreement to be the best parents for our son. The meeting with the pastor, who became our mediator, was actually peaceful. He was there to assist us to begin our separation with clarity and understanding. Our agreement was to be the best parents for our son. The meeting went well because we had no arguments or hostile attitudes toward each other. That night ended on a peaceful note.

The next day, I got up feeling refreshed. I was satisfied that one chapter was closed with the understanding that another mountain must be climbed. I put on my new uniform for work and headed out the door. As I closed the door behind me, my life was turned upside down. I didn't realize that once I got up early that morning to prepare for work I was going to be faced with major obstacles in life. I didn't think that as I opened the door something different was going to happen to me. That morning when I opened the door, I had a gun in my face. The man in black pointing the gun at me then told me to get in the car. He then attacked me by shooting at me four times. The man in black was my husband.

I was rushed to the hospital and was told that I had a paralysis and may not be able to walk again. Family and friends prayed for me; however, you always get someone that says, "Now you know you have to forgive the person." Now it is very hard to agree to forgive when you are facing a major physical change in your body.

Let's be real—having a paralysis doesn't just mean unable to walk again. In my situation, it also meant that I was unable to go to the bathroom the same way and had to take care of things differently. As time went by, I learned more about my body and rebuilt my confidence. I thought that two years after the attack I would have a better understanding of how to forgive, but I wasn't there yet. I wanted to go back to my mother's old residence, but I couldn't.

A few years went by, and I actually took a ride to the area where the attack happened. The grounds were turned over because there was a water main leak where a pipe burst in the condominium complex. I said a prayer and was able to bury all the hate in the soil that was exposed. This particular prayer was the start of the true healing process of forgiveness. I thank God for allowing me to be able to forgive. One must understand that it takes time, patience, and understanding. It took time for me to find myself spiritually, physically, and emotionally, not just as an individual, not just as a woman, but as a mother.

When trying to think about how to forgive, it helped me to think about why and what I am really forgiving him for. Now this is where I had to really get out of my own self and look at the situation from an outsider's perspective. I actually did think about his upbringing and try to see where this behavior came from, not to excuse this evil spirit and inhuman actions, but to learn through the pain of this madness. We may never know the origin of this behavior, but we must try. We as a people identify love differently. However, we must understand empathy as part of the human experience. If you're lacking empathy, I believe it's hard to be conscious of humanity.

Sometimes we don't understand why we get in these relationships. The one thing I do want to say is that some of our relationships are actually what I call "therapeutic relationships." Over the years, I've relearned that we are supposed to learn these missing channels that we are lacking within ourselves and help each other grow. As friends or partners, we should learn to be comfortable and vulnerable enough within the safe space with someone in the "relationship." Sadly, we don't always get to that part in our relationships. I had to really think about this in various directions. We don't know what others are fighting mentally. I'm not giving him an excuse for his decisions at all. I just had to pray that even though I will never know what his battles were and his true cause for his catastrophic decision, my son and I find peace.

Just moments after I was able to forgive, I felt the weight lift off my shoulders. I felt lighter in my heart. I felt lighter in my spirit. I felt breath. There was new breath in my soul, and days after, weeks after, months after, and years after, I began to be able to smile more internally. I was able to take off my mask and actually feel great about myself as a woman with a spinal cord injury. With God's guidance, I started to live more in my truth and my purpose. I am Sunshine King who learned how to forgive.

Exiting Your Dark Places

Tunisia J. L. Patel

I think it's safe to say that we all have something good within us; something powerful; something amazing; something useful to even potentially change the world, or at least the neighborhood. That includes you. Yes, really. Certainly, your life here on this earth is no mistake and even if you simply cannot see it, it's true. There's a gift within. This has been a rehearsed conversation and expectation throughout all of my life beginning as a child. If you're anything like me, you bought into this conversation also. You and I, we believe in our gifts. We believe in that gift that is inside us.

We say, "I'm gifted, and I'm going to do big things in life!" Be honest. You've said it before. Perhaps not in those exact words, but close enough. Maybe you were off to be the first college graduate in your family. Maybe you began the race to be the first successful business owner among your peers. Wait, could it be the plan to travel the world and become a political or public figure helping any and every breathing creature? Regardless of what the big thing was, like Superman whisking up in the air fist first, off you went!

Trust me. I know the feeling of whisking up in the air ready to be some form of a hero to anything or anyone needing saving. What I was not aware of was the storms that occur beyond that wonderful, powerful whisk. You know, the thunder, the flashing, and the lightening. These storms in life teach us (heroes) a very powerful lesson about the gift of forgiveness. While some gifts are unwrapped, other gifts must be unlocked. So, let our journey begin.

It was as if I had walked into a room, closed the door behind me, and turned the lights out for good. I had lost everything. In 2013, I lost my job after seven years of working at a company. I actually loved that job at one point, but it was gone. A few months later, my husband lost his job of several years. The house on the hill (literally) was gone two months later. Now, it seemed as though it was the car's turn to go, which it did one month later. After each loss, I held it together pretty well as I continued to go about life and do whatever I had the capacity to do at that point. My husband and I were basically homeless for nearly 18 months with two homes that provided temporary emergency shelter here and there.

I was so ashamed of my storm. I was hurting deep for so many more reasons than this alone. The lights were out, and life was now dark to me. Have you ever hit what you thought was rock bottom and refused to look at anything but the rock and the bottom? Were you really still "all in" on the conversation of the gift within you? Well, not me. It was difficult, even though I attempted to maintain life and smile from time to time. The inability to forgive was turning into bitterness and smashing my gift. The last straw had to be booking hotel rooms to have a bed and shower every one, two, or three nights at a time.

During this time, I had seemingly boxed up my gift, taped it with packing tape, stapled the ribbons down, and thrown it on a shelf never to be used. Forget about business. Give up on school. Nothing else matters anymore! I'm not meant to be anything or anybody! These are lies I entertained. I was yelling in this dark place, but no one could hear me. I was resentful about the fact that people had no idea what was going on. Let's just ignore the fact that I sort of didn't tell them either. I was mad that there was no BFF to call. I was mad at my husband for any and everything that had happened, and although we were in this together, it was a bit miserable at times. Everything in life that went wrong, in my opinion, was everyone else's fault. It must have been the "they and them" syndrome. The people I wanted to be there were not. The people I had no idea would be there were there. The thunder and lightning in the storm brought with it voices that lied to me, belittled me, excluded me, hated me, looked over me, stepped over me, blocked me, ignored me, forgot about me, and the list goes on.

Do you realize that staying in such a dark place can do some serious damage to your gift?

A scripture that comes to mind would be, "For I reckon that the sufferings of this present time are not worthy to be compared with the glory which shall be revealed in us" (Romans 8:18, KJV).

I decree this day that that gift in you will survive and thrive beyond your dark place. I further declare an exit from your dark place in this very season! I understand your situations did happen. Family failed you. Friends disappointed you. Life hit hard and even threw you for a loopy loo. Yet one of the lessons I learned is that "life goes on." I suppose it would be nice for the entire world to stop and attend to our personal crisis, but never has there been a day for that to occur. At least not for you and me. Friend, I really had to think. Yes, it happened, but the real question is: what happens next? If something different doesn't happen, and I mean fast, this gift that people open will be corroded, decayed, and just a mess!

SOMEBODY, PLEASE HELP ME. I'M GIFTED, BUT MY GIFT IS ON LOCK!

I'm glad you called out for help because it is one of the things I had to do to exit my dark place. Since we're here now, let's go ahead and do some work. There was no doubt in my mind that God had placed in me some major gifting and abilities. They meant nothing if I chose to remain in a dark place. No one would ever see nor benefit from the gifts. So, the first thing that helped me come to myself was seeing the possibilities through the lives of those who were whisking. Here is your "Dark Place Exit Plan."

1. **Look Up and Around.** Funny things happen in dark places. My ability to dream and have clear vision was affected, but God strengthened my head to lift up just a little. I saw others moving forward and pursuing purpose. I saw people making big moves and attempts at success. Seeing life moving on and forward in others' lives sparked something in me. Hope was budding. You need to first look up and around.

2. **Acknowledge the You in the Dark Place.** There came a moment when I realized that the only one in my dark place was me. I had to admit that even if the pain of this place was real, it was me standing in need of help. The blame game had to stop and healing had to start.

3. **Seek Wise Counsel.** I get it. No one else knew it, but I had become ill, and both my heart and soul were sick. I looked for trusted, unbiased, professional help. Learning the commonality of my situation and knowing that how I felt was normal but not required was a relief. You must talk it through and get a right perspective.

4. **Let It Go! Let Them Go!** This is where light starts to shine in a little so you can get to that exit. Don't forget your gift though. It's on the shelf, remember? Go get it, and make a decision.

Release every feeling of resentment and offense. Tears may flow, but you're on your way to that exit from your dark place. Release those hostages in your heart. The gift allows you to have freedom, and no one owes you anything anymore! You're debt free, and so are they. Head to the door, turn that light switch on and exit now.

5. **Open Your G.I.F.T.S.** Share them with the world. Now that all of that corrosion and decay is gone, you have so much more to give!

Your experiences were actually all ordained. You had to experience the most difficult times in your life for a reason, and no one can show others out of dark places like we can. This is truly a "been there done that" experience. At the end of the day, there are millions of individuals, operating in the very opposing activity of their gifts, leaving them to remain in dark places, never tapping inside. You will not be one of them now. In fact, I believe you are going to help them, because you have exited your dark place.

Triumph

Choosing the Right Path for Your Life

Cynthia McCalister

You always have choices in life. When you get to a fork in the road of your journey, it is up to you to choose the right path. My name is Cynthia McCalister. I have been a leader working in Information Technology for over 20 years. I am also the owner of an IT Company, Quality SAP, a certified minority and woman-owned business. Why is this introduction important? Women make up about 25 percent of employees in information technology. African American women represent three percent of employees working in technology (Women in Tech, 2016). There are few African American and female-owned information technology companies in this country—the percentage is less than one percent (US Equal Employment Opportunity Commission, 2015). My G.I.F.T. is that of "triumph," which has allowed me to get where I am today. My journey is that of inspiration, but it was not an easy path. I would not have achieved so much if it was not for my faith in God, the support of my family, and following my dream.

I was influenced by my parents, Thomas and Madlyn Johnson. They gave me the drive to be an entrepreneur. I was born in Akron, Ohio, but shortly after birth, my family moved to Puerto Rico. My father had been working as an air traffic controller, an occupation for which he trained while in the Air Force. We lived in Puerto Rico for over two years. After that period, we moved to Daytona Beach, Florida. In the early eighties, the air traffic controllers implemented a strike that was broken by the Reagan administration. My father and all of his co-workers on strike were terminated. This was a devastating event for my family. It caused my father to re-evaluate what was next for him and my family. After being laid off as an air traffic controller, my father set out on a new path to start his own business, Regal Carpet Cleaning, and become a small business owner. My family of five was very close. We all supported each other and my father's dream. We were hands on in the business, helping with tasks, learning, and participating in duties as assigned. I saw firsthand both the ups and downs of being an entrepreneur through his journey, which had a strong impact on me. I was able to see the possibilities of being your own boss.

As a child, I always had a gift for fixing things and wanting to create and invent. I excelled in math and would spend time working on creations, building ideas, and cultivating my curiosity about technology. I knew at a young age that engineering and technology would be my career path.

It was a great experience living in Puerto Rico and Florida and growing up around a variety of cultures and languages. After my parents had been away from their childhood home of Dayton, Ohio for many years, they finally decided to move back in 1989. I had never seen snow, so living in Ohio was a big change to me. We ended up living in the same house my mom and dad bought when they first got married. It stayed in the family with my uncle. For me, the move to Dayton was a period of adjustment to a new life and of getting to know extended family whom I had only seen on yearly visits. My father was working to establish his business in Ohio.

We were only in Dayton for six months when we received an early morning phone call from the hospital. It was just two days before my 13th. birthday. I was the one who picked up the phone. We found out that my father had collapsed and died while at work. That was a pivotal moment in my life. It set the stage for my gift of "triumph" to come to light. I was an adolescent in a new place who had just lost the foundation of the family. When you lose someone you love so much, it is hard to move forward. As a teenager who had just lost her father, I could have easily decided to hate the world and act out from my pain and grief. Instead, I made a vow to myself to not let my father's lessons and faith in my dreams go to waste. I was determined to work hard, stay focused in school, and get my degree in engineering.

After my father's passing, my mom, my sisters, and I spent more time with our extended family for support. My mom restarted her career and chose to focus on areas of community outreach. She became a drug and alcohol abuse counselor. She worked for the AIDS Foundation of Dayton, putting on events and bringing awareness. She later became a minister and was a staple in the community with her service and work. As a teenager, I would always be there to support her and help her with her programs. Her passion and the impact she had on others instilled in me the importance of giving back and supporting the community.

As a student, I attended an engineering magnet high school, which was also where I met my future husband. I ended up graduating with high honors and receiving a scholarship to Wright State University, which was also where my father went to college. I was a direct admit into the College of Engineering and one of very few African American females in the program. Most of my time in college was spent in the lab studying. My introduction to information technology came when I was admitted into INROADS, a wonderful program that helped to develop and place top minority youth in business and industry. I began my career path working as an intern in information technology at Procter and Gamble, which later resulted in full-time employment upon graduating from college. I was the only African American female in my graduating class to graduate with a degree in electrical engineering.

After spending years working for large IT corporations, I made the decision, supported by my family, to venture out on my own and start my business. Quality SAP was established in 2007. I started my business because of my passion to use my talents to make a positive impact on the lives of others. I wanted to build a corporation that would provide technology to support growth for small businesses. In addition, I wanted to offer programs to introduce and provide opportunities for others to enter the world of technology while cultivating programs to support positive causes in the community.

Quality SAP stands for Quality, Service, and Products. It is a thriving Information Technology company specializing in mobile application development. One great product we offer is the Key Spot (www.keyspot.com) mobile application platform. Key Spot is utilized by business owners across the country. It is an ideal tool for businesses to market, promote, and communicate their products and services. It offers an affordable way to leverage mobile technology and share information within the community.

Quality SAP is more than a technology company. We utilize a network to support small businesses and help them thrive. When I get comments from small business owners such as "Thank you for your support and for all you do for my business!" or "Thank you! You really help keep me going!" the hard work put into running my businesses is all worth it to me. According to the Small Business Association statistics of 2015, about 50 percent of businesses fail in their first year. I want to believe my efforts can make a difference, one business owner at a time. So, for any business looking for support and growth, join the Key Spot family. Visit www.keyspotapp.com.

It is my mission to support others looking to build their business and give back to the community. These were lessons instilled within me from a young age. I saw firsthand the hard work my father put into growing his business. With my mother, I saw God's love demonstrated by her work in the community. In March 2012 (just two days after my father's birthday), my cheerleader in life, my mom, passed away. She went on to be with her love, my father. It was a terrible and sudden loss for me, my family, and my siblings. For her funeral, the building was overflowing with the many people she had touched. With courage, I stood up and spoke, sharing how I would continue on her path of giving back to the community. Though my parents are no longer with us, their legacy lives on through me, as I continue my work helping others achieve their business dreams while being a positive light in the community.

God's Time Is the Perfect Time!

Arlene Foster

GIFT:
TRIUMPH

There are numerous testimonies of triumphs of the human spirit from people who have endured and overcome horrific situations in their lives. Oftentimes, these wounded people have gone on to make significant contributions to our society as accomplished entrepreneurs, writers, actors, politicians, and activists. Many have credited their misfortunes as the catalyst that propelled them toward success. I have always been fascinated and in awe of such stories and a bit perplexed by their motivation and determination, which led me to ask the question, "Why can't I get my act together?"

I had a wonderful, happy, relatively drama-free childhood filled with love and familial support. I came from a working-class nuclear family. My father worked for a small family-owned business, and my mother was a homemaker who provided childcare in our home. They were married sixty-three years when my father passed.

In many ways, we were the Huxtables, minus the wealth. Both of my parents had a strong faith in God, and they passed this on to their children. They spent quality time together celebrating family traditions and supporting the family unit. Our home was a haven filled with love, joy, laughter, and happiness. Life was great. Not perfect, but great!

You would think with so much stability in my life and so few obstacles that carving out a path for my future would have been a piece of cake. But au contraire, trying to figure out what I wanted to be when I grew up became a perennial thorn in my side. Without a clear focus after high school, I decided to join the workforce upon graduation and swiftly landed a well-paying job in Corporate America. What more could a girl ask for? I had a good job, a loving family, great friends, and a nice bank account. Life was an endless party. But, despite my good fortune, there was a nagging void that I could not identify. Eager to find a solution, I opted for higher learning. Maybe furthering my education would do the trick!

Devoid of clarity, I entered evening classes and followed the advice of my high school guidance counselor who suggested I pursue the wave of the future, and in the eighties, that meant entering the field of computer science. I quickly realized that technology was not a wave I wanted to ride, so as the surfers say, I bailed out.

In my mid to late twenties, I began what would become my rollercoaster of a life. This is the ride of events that takes you to an exhilarating high and then suddenly drops you into an abyss. Everyone at some point has been on this path of twists and turns and ups and downs. My journey consisted of marriage, job promotions, miscarriages, infertility struggles, high-risk pregnancies, and the birth of three beautiful children. It also included a corporate lawsuit for discrimination, exciting career changes, a devastating and debilitating illness of my spouse, financial ruin, and miraculous recovery. I have mourned the death of my father, family members, and friends. I have celebrated my mother's ninetieth birthday, educational accomplishments, and an extraordinary opportunity to become an author. But most importantly, I re-established a relationship with God.

Still, as I forged ahead in life, that nagging feeling of discontent periodically resurfaced. Eventually, I realized that feeling had a name. It was called purpose. That epiphany led me on a quest to seek God's perfect will for my life, and He began to reveal His purpose and plan. Not knowing my purpose caused me many years of frustration. At times, it felt like my life had been for naught, knowing that my God-given talents weren't being utilized. I received another revelation as well. God inspired me to change my focus from trying to figure out what I wanted to be to discovering who I was created to be, even though the days of my youth had passed. That was the point where I began to reconcile that the journey I was on was in accordance with God's timeline and not a natural schedule.

"Do not conform to the pattern of this world, but
be transformed by the renewing of your mind. Then
you will be able to test and approve what God's will
is—his good, pleasing and perfect will."
—Romans 12:2 (NIV)

God also reassured me that my experiences had not been in vain. The process was coming together just as He had planned. He had to shape, mold, and perfect me, just as the potter does with clay. He was firing clay from mud to ceramic, converting the weak clay into a strong, durable masterpiece. He needed to perform the ceramic change: the slow, fiery process of clay becoming ceramic. Once this change occurs, it cannot be reversed. I realize that there is still more sanding and grinding before the process is complete; but, in the end, God will have created a vessel for His special purposes, made holy, useful to the Master and prepared to do any good work. I am grateful for His process.

"But thanks be to God, who always leads us in
triumph in Christ, and through us spreads and
makes evident everywhere the sweet fragrance of
the knowledge of Him."
—2 Corinthians 2:14 (AMP)

My advice for those who are searching for their purpose is to not criticize yourself for what you feel you haven't accomplished or for what may appear to be wasted time. Don't discount the things that seem small or insignificant. Recognize and acknowledge those moments, because there is purpose in all things.

One of my favorite Christmas movies is *It's a Wonderful Life*. In the movie, the main character falls on hard times, gets discouraged, and wishes he had never been born. An angel grants his wish, and he soon discovers the magnitude of how he has changed and impacted the lives of many. Their lives would have been much different had they not had an encounter with him. So, embrace every encounter because you never know the significant impact of your presence.

I have been blessed to have an arsenal of family and friends who have been supportive throughout my pilgrimage, and the assembly has continued to grow. Ask God for discernment concerning the people who are in your circle because everyone may not support your dreams, and dream killers are the last thing you need on your spiritual and purpose-seeking journey. It is critical to surround yourself with people who have your best interests at heart, who exude positive energy, and who provide nuggets of wisdom and constructive criticism. Establish connections with people who are nurturing, and who can help you grow and flourish. In turn, you will be able to pay it forward with those invaluable gems.

Most importantly, don't focus on your age or how long it will take to achieve a goal. We often talk ourselves out of doing great things by saying, "I'll be forty-five or sixty-two by the time I finish." A close friend of mine would always say, "You're going to be that age whether you do it or not. So, why not do it?" God can use anyone at any age. Moses, Aaron, Joshua, and Anna are a testament to that.

Your personal journey is essential to your specific purpose and destiny. Never believe it is too late to discover your dream. Don't ever believe it's too late to walk in your calling. Seek God's guidance, glean His wisdom, and be encouraged in knowing that God's time is the perfect time. God's mission for you is precise and intentional. Only you can execute His plan.

"'For I know the plans I have for you,' declares the Lord, 'plans to prosper you and not to harm you, plans to give you hope and a future. Then you will call on me and come and pray to me, and I will listen to you. You will seek me and find me when you seek me with all your heart."
—Jeremiah 29:11-13 (NIV)

Road to the Dream

Aurea McGarry

GIFT:
TRIUMPH

Walking the red carpet in a gorgeous, floor-length, form-fitting, designer gown surrounded by family and friends with a handsome, loving husband by her side and winning a golden statue for being outstanding in the entertainment industry is many little girls' dream. It was mine too. "I'd like to thank the Academy!" was all I wanted to grow up to say as my agent would excitingly schedule me to sit on Johnny Carson's couch the following night to talk to me about my success and how it felt to win the highest award in the business.

"You're crazy!" "That's an impossible dream!" "It's who you know and who you do favors for in Hollywood to ever make it big." Those are the words young girls would hear growing up as well-meaning adults would tell them to go to college and get a real job. Which is certainly not bad advice. And trust me, I did try that route, but my journey to a practical life got derailed many times and took me straight toward my so-called crazy, impossible little girl dream. But by no means was the road smooth.

Throughout my childhood in Manhattan, I was surrounded by the sparkling lights of Broadway, TV studios lining the streets, and celebrities passing me by on every corner (and many living in my Upper East Side apartment building too). Show business was all around me, and I had the most amazing mother who always told me I was beautiful and could do anything in this world that I wanted to do. I never believed the part about me being beautiful. I was a tomboy at heart, and she was by far the most beautiful woman I'd ever seen. She was a former commercial model in the 1950s with the iconic 18-inch waist, long legs, the perfect nose, long, golden-blonde hair, and blue eyes. Heads turned everywhere she went. She loved every bit of it and the glamorous lifestyle her multimillion-dollar Greek tycoon husband provided for her and her three children. It was the perfect environment for me to have the award-winning dreams that I had. I was born in the right city with the right parents who encouraged me and sent me to the best schools, and I had everything an aspiring young actress could ever want and more. A perfect recipe for success.

Well, life is never perfect. And looking back now, I wouldn't want it to be. I've learned more through my struggles than my triumphs, and when life turns up the heat, the real triumphs can happen. Your inner "tea bag" gets stronger, and the waters get hotter. And my waters got hot!

My silver-spoon lifestyle came crashing down piece by piece over many years. It all started when I turned 15 and my father was murdered. He was shot three times in the head while on a business trip in Boston. We came to find out that this was a planned event by organized criminals who wanted my brilliant and successful Dad dead and out of their way. My mother had divorced him several years prior to his death, but he kept us all in the lifestyle to which we had grown accustomed and we saw him as often as his busy career as an attorney and investment banker would allow. This event began the hot water flowing into my perfect young life, and what happened in the next forty years would be nothing short of miraculous.

As the floodgates of my new realty without a father providing for my every need set in, I didn't lose faith in my Hollywood dreams. I was young and invincible. After grieving the loss, I still stood strong, lied about my age, and got a job at 15 in a local Irish pub making $400+ a day working Saturday and Sunday brunches, paying for my private high school for young actors and dance classes on Broadway. I was also able to pay the mortgage on our new high-rise apartment my mom and I moved into after not being able to afford the other apartment in which we once lived. Thankfully, it was still very nice and only six blocks north of where we had been.

I was so determined to make a living now and help my mom that I graduated early at 16 and jumped right into the adult world of working and paying bills. I did immediately go on to attend a year at Marymount Manhattan

College and then went to the New York Academy of Theatrical Arts. I never missed a beat working weekends, going to school, auditioning for everything in *Variety Magazine* for which I was a fit (including the movie production of *Hair*), and surviving my new life. I discovered I loved working and being busy, which I now know is a character trait that is still serving me very well to this day.

I would love to tell you that all went great after I bounced back from the murder of my father, but as you can imagine, it was only the beginning of my obstacles and the depth of strength I would discover inside myself and build upon each day from that moment on. The road to my red carpet night took many deep and dark twist and turns. I had long lost my little girl dream many times when I unknowingly married an abusive man and when I lost my mother to the horrific disease of liver and lung cancer, which killed her only five months after her diagnoses. Her death left me crushed beyond my wildest dreams, as I lost my lifetime best friend. Not a day goes by without wanting to see her beautiful face again and hear her voice telling me, "You can do anything you want to in this world, Sweetheart." Unfortunately, this was not the end of cancer striking my life, as a few years later, my brother got it. Thankfully, he survived. A few months after that, the doctors told me that I, too, have cancer.

By the time I was diagnosed, I was 32 and divorced from my abusive husband but had a beautiful daughter who was then 13 and about to watch her mother go through the battle of her lifetime over non-Hodgkin's lymphoma. God is so good, though, and didn't allow us to go through this life-threatening adventure alone. Three years before my cancer battle, I married my Prince Charming, Brian McGarry, who never wavered once throughout the storms. My cancer battle has been the hardest road I have ever walked, but it's also been the road to triumph in a monumental way. It has given me and my family our life's work—a legacy to live!

During my cancer surgery in 1999, the doctors needed to be confident that they removed all the cancer cells humanly possible out of my body to allow the chemo to then sweep up the rest. So, they removed my thymus gland, half of my left lung, part of my right lung, the lining around my heart, and the left nerve to my vocal cord and disconnected half of my diaphragm. They told me I would never speak above a very faint whisper ever again—that it would be **impossible**. End of story and the end of my red carpet dreams? Absolutely not. Where there is faith, there is hope and a future. It just may look and *sound* different from first imagined, but being flexible and willing to ride the tides and keep my heart and eye on my dreams has made a world of difference. The journey may change, but the goal remains unharmed.

In 2010, I cried tears of joy sitting at a beautifully adorned round gala table with Brian and my family and friends dressed in elegant, formal attire as we all screamed and shouted when the on-stage presenter spoke the famous words that I spent a lifetime dreaming about but thought would elude me forever. "And the Emmy

Award goes to… Aurea McGarry!!!!" Shocked, weak at the knees, and barely able to grab my husband's hand, we walked together through the crowded room of fellow TV professionals to the spectacular stage to accept my golden statue award and to tell the audience that their dreams can come true. Because if I just won the highest award in the land for having a television talk show and I should not be able to talk, then my God, what is stopping you from your dreams coming true, no matter what your age or circumstances are?

As I returned to my chair, my friend reached over to me and said, "Your mother would be proud!" This statement made that night even more special as my little girl dream came true in the most unconventional, miraculous way after hell and high waters tried to stop it.

Won't you join me and be unstoppable!

How I Became a Published Author on the Run

Blaque Diamond

I'm not going to tell you a story, but what I will do is take you on a journey. According to Frank Sinatra, "If you can make it here, you can make it anywhere." Well, I guess I couldn't make it in New York because I left right after 911. Not the 911 America has come to know, but this 911.

We relocated hoping to start life over and leave our worries behind, but after five years living in another state and three weeks of pure hell, we went into hiding. At that point, I only had two questions I needed answered. The first question I asked myself was: Why didn't I go to college after high school? The other question: Why me, God?

Everyone had just moved out of the house—my mother, sister, nieces, nephews, and even my brother and his girlfriend were gone. We were all living in my mother's house. My husband and I were about to remodel the house when our world turned upside down. I never thought that a hit would be put out on my family and me. Why? My family and I were in the way of someone's business that could make them a lot of money. I was led to believe that a relative wanted my husband, my children, and me to disappear; so, we packed up what we could and headed south. South was just three hours away and as far as our money would take us. After six days in another state, I wondered if we made the right decision; my family was homeless due to our slumlord. The place was full of rats, there was a draft coming through the windows, and the back door was not secure.

We both were able to find employment, and I was even able to find a second job and enroll part-time at an HBCU. So, after working hard and saving a few dollars, we decided to purchase a house. But the more money we collected, the more my husband drank. One minute we were all lovey-dovey, and the next minute, all hell was breaking loose in our marriage. I'll never forget the time my husband swore at me and the first time I threw a Pepsi bottle at him. Sometimes we would argue because he was gone overnight without any mention as to where he was. It was becoming such a habit that I stopped asking where he was; my focus was the kids, work, and school. And when he did come home, it was the same thing all over again. The mere mention of him going into rehab began a whole new argument.

The next day while at work, I received a phone call that the ambulance rushed my husband to the hospital. The nurse said he was so drunk that he didn't know where he was or that he had had a stroke. When I arrived, the doctors said the treatment was crucial, and my husband would need to remain in the hospital. When asked what caused his stroke, I was informed that he was under stress at home and that I needed to be a bit more patient with him. Now wait a minute. I'm working two jobs, going to college, and raising the kids, and he's stressed out? Give me a break! I am trying my best not to lose my mind and continue to love him at the same time, but he is not making being married to him easy.

He came home about a week later, barely able to move the left side of his body. My husband had problems speaking, and his ability to feel the right side of his body was limited. I'll admit there were times I wanted to walk away, but I stayed for two reasons: I didn't know where I would go and I adored my husband.

He was barely out of the hospital before he started drinking and smoking cigarettes again. I knew he was smoking when I saw smoke floating out the bedroom window and cigarette butts on the ground below the window. He tried telling me that the smoke in the bedroom was from the neighbors barbecuing. Really? A bbq in October? Not to mention I found a couple of bottles of Jack Daniels hidden under the cedar chest in the closet.

I don't know how my husband was getting the cigarettes and the liquor, but what I do know is that this man had a death wish. He wasn't listening to anything the doctor told him. I remember telling my husband that enough was enough and that I was tired of his behavior. Of course, my husband made this about me; he said I didn't understand what he was going through and that he needed answers as to why he was adopted. As I turned to go downstairs, he jumped up and walked quickly behind me. My husband told me that he was leaving and that he didn't know when he would be back. I warned him that if he continued to drink and not take care of himself as the doctor said, someday he would drop dead.

We buried my husband on December 9, but he passed away on November 15. For three weeks, I searched for him. And for three weeks, he lay on a slab with a body tag at the medical examiner's office as an unknown. It wasn't like him to be gone so long, not to mention he didn't cash his social security check. We searched under the freeway, walked through Tent City, and called the hospitals and homeless shelters. We even checked correctional facilities. No one had seen him. It took everything I had before calling the morgue, and there he was, identified by the same tattoo I wished he had never gotten; the one with her initials on his shoulder.

Later that day, I requested his belongings from the hospital and was informed that the hospital could not release his things to me because of HIPAA. The only way the hospital would release his belongings to me was if the medical examiner (ME) agreed. Well, I picked up his belongings after the ME accepted my request, only to find in his wallet his ID, my son's medical assistance card, and my phone number behind the picture of a little girl from the homeless shelter where he was living. The hospital said the cause of death was a heart attack, but the autopsy reported it was a cardiac arrest. At this point, I didn't believe anything the hospital had to say. First of all, there's a difference between a heart attack and cardiac arrest. But furthermore, I still did not know why he was in the morgue for three weeks without them notifying me. My husband had identification on him.

Just when things couldn't get any worse, about six months after burying my husband, my family and I witnessed a murder. The authorities said they were moving my family to an undisclosed location and that we had 30 minutes to get in and to get out of the house with whatever we needed. I remember we were barely in the home before we escaped a near home explosion; someone had broken into the house and left the gas turned on. Also, the thermostat was not intact. The light was flickering and the mercury was exposed, so we abandoned everything we had.

Ninety-nine years without the possibility of parole. That's what the man who shot the teenager got, and we were free to live our lives. It's been almost 12 years since I buried my husband. When he died, I remembered feeling numb from the brain down. Until this day, I still hold on to his bloodstained pants, his wallet, and his ID.

It may not bring me closure, but it bears me closeness. I often wonder what I could have done that would have stopped him from walking out the door that last night. I thought I was supposed to spend the rest of my life with him, but he spent the rest of his life with me.

Although I may never learn the truth about my husband's death, and he may never know his reality, what I do know is the answer to my question: Why me, God? He chose me so I can advocate for people like my husband by providing an incessantly endless passage for foster or adoptive children who would like to gain insight into their journey.

Being Brown in a Black and White World

Dr. Angela Kenzslowe

GIFT:
TRIUMPH

I felt empty—a feeling that my roots were a false pretense of my existence. I was being forced to move beyond my desire to create a great life for my child. I had to look toward my past and understand that reflection is an opportunity for growth. This journey allowed me to realize that triumph is more than not wanting to be like those that came before me. Being able to be triumphant is a compilation of experiences, family history, close friends, and spirituality.

I was born into this world in 1971. The U.S. Supreme Court had deemed interracial marriages legal just five years prior. I wasn't a legal crime, but to some, I was worse. On my birth certificate, my father was listed as Negro and my mother was listed as Caucasian. There was no race classification for me. This was the beginning of a lifelong intrigue with race and where I fit.

THE EARLY YEARS

The day I was born, my mother's brother stopped speaking to her because she had a "nigger" baby. My birth was a large rift in her family. She's from a middle-class white family and wasn't allowed to have black friends. My grandfather was forced to accept me. I have fond memories of him and my grandmother around my kindergarten year. My grandma would walk me to the school bus stop. Grandpa would tickle me. I have memories of eating at the table as a family and doing fun things. I also have memories of my father's family during my early life. I remember my uncle riding me on his bike and another time pulling me on a sled in the snow. My father was also raised in a well-to-do family with his parents and siblings.

My parents separated around 1974. In 1977, my life would change and my loss of identity would begin. My father died. A few months later, my mother had a son with another man. Having a second bi-racial child was not acceptable to my grandfather, so he disowned my mother, my brother, and me. Because of distance, we lost touch with my father's family. Then my brother's father left a year after he was born. It was my mother, brother, and me left to conquer the world.

A NEW LIFE

Our new life separate from family, traditions, support, and love was upon us. My mother was challenged to create something new—a foundation and a wall of security. She was a widowed white woman in the 1970s with two bi-racial children and only a 12th-grade education. My mother carried a strong burden to make life choices that would enable us to survive. She refused to use federal welfare funds to support us, although she did receive survivor's social security due to my father's early death. She did what she could to ensure we lived in neighborhoods that were safe. We would go to "the camping food store" where we would get half a dozen eggs, powdered milk, and a huge block of cheese. After leaving the "camping food store," we'd camp. We would swim in the lake, hike, and look for snakes. We would fish. Yep, I can hook a worm and clean a fish. I can tell you, cleaning the fish always grossed me out a bit. We would cook on the camp fire. I loved to camp and always looked forward to it. When we were done camping, we always lived someplace new. It was a new adventure. New neighbors, new kids to play with, and sometimes even a new school in a new town. What I didn't realize until I was older was that we camped because we were homeless.

Her tenacity to keep us oblivious of our true hardships is one of the most commendable traits my mother has. My mother taught me that I could create my own reality. I took this lesson to heart and continued to teach it to my son and grandchildren.

ADOPTED FAMILY

Although I was not connected to my biological extended family during childhood and adolescence, my mother did connect us to her best friend. I grew up calling my mother's best friend my aunt and adopted her family as my own. Aunt T., as I affectionately called her, was Filipina and West Indian. She, too, was biracial and had four children with fathers from various racial backgrounds. My new family was mixed with brown, black, and white people. I had a family that embraced everyone, including me.

I learned from my Aunt T. that we can love and live with all people. I learned from her that although I did not have her blood, I was her family. I learned that love and family transcend blood ties and race. Aunt T. taught me how to love myself even when others chose not to love me. She taught me that it takes a village to raise a child.

COMMUNITY

In addition to the lessons I learned from growing up with my adopted family, I was highly influenced by those who were in my community. I lived the majority of my adolescent years in southern San Diego, where we resided closer to downtown Tijuana, Mexico, than downtown San

Diego. Everyone within my community was brown— Filipino, Mexican, Chamorro, Samoan, Hawaiian, black, and of course, white people with tans. Race was not an issue. We embraced one another with open arms. I was a Dama in two quinceañeras, ate spam and rice for breakfast, had pork chops at home, and understood whose house to take my shoes off in and whose home to keep them on in. English, Spanish, and Tagalog were the main languages with which we all became familiar.

This experience allowed me to live in a cultural bubble that did not exist outside of our community. Once I left San Diego and moved to Arizona, the questions began. "What are you?" "What do you claim?" White people at my new school did not like me because I was not white, and black girls did not accept me because I was "light." I was 16, away from everyone and everything I knew, and was being asked questions to which I did not have answers. Confusion settled in. I could not "pass" for white and did not want to be forced to pass for only black as history and social norms dictated. I could no longer just be brown. I had to choose.

Anytown, USA

A school counselor was aware of the struggles I was enduring in the new environment and gave me a scholarship to attend a diversity camp called Anytown, USA. Anytown addresses prejudice and social identity groups and offers a safe place to share and learn with one another. As a delegate, I participated in focused dialogue groups to help develop understanding of myself, how I fit with the larger community, friends, and family, and how to identify things that made those relationships meaningful. I wholeheartedly say that Anytown changed my life. I was able to explore my family dynamics with my mother's father being racist and not having adequate contact with my father's family. I was introduced to various faith systems and realized spirituality was missing in my life. I could be me, whatever that was, without having to have a label from someone else.

CURRENTLY ME

Many people who know me now do not know the struggles I had growing up. I took what my mother taught me with her fortitude and strong work ethic and was able to move beyond poverty and into middle-class life, where she started. I believe part of my desire to do well was to prove to my mother's father that I was able to "make something" of myself. Being "not white" would not hinder me from doing well. I no longer live to prove him wrong. I love life and have so much more to live.

CONCLUSION

I feel blessed for the advantage of having grown up biracial in a culturally mixed environment. The community where I grew up did not force me to make a choice or to even recognize that a choice had to be made.

Growing up as I did has provided me the opportunity to embrace people with various ethnic backgrounds, cultural heritages, and spiritual beliefs. Early in life, I was exposed to both the horrific ideals as well as beautiful embraces with which some greet biracial people. This self-exploration was a definite challenge as I took for granted my exposure to diverse lifestyles. I believed culture was specific to ethnic and racial divisions and thought I was missing that element in my life. I learned that my culture is one of acceptance, thoughts of wellness, and personal responsibility while still being part of an extended family. I do not exist to refute others' beliefs of me; I exist to embrace my beliefs of myself.

I am black AND white. I am biracial. I am triumphant.

Perseverance: The Gateway to Triumph

Ericka L. McKnight

GIFT:

TRIUMPH

"What we do not see, what most of us never suspect of existing, is the silent but irresistible power which comes to the rescue of those who fight on in the face of discouragement."
—Napoleon Hill

I am a bestselling author, speaker, CEO of ELM Realty, and a philanthropist. Even though these successes were great achievements, my mind, soul, body, and spirit still felt hungry for greatness. Have you ever been there? So, I began to write down my next endeavor to open a real estate school in the Carolinas. This was so much bigger than me because I'd never taught before and had no knowledge of the process or how this greater idea was going to come together. But I couldn't allow all these uncertainties to block my path of perseverance.

My first step in the process was to write a real estate continuing education course to be approved by the North and South Carolina Real Estate Commissions. The required outline, format, and topics/subject matter appeared on paper to be out of my league, which was very intimidating. Yet I was determined to create greatness in my life. After two painful rejections of my course, I felt like a failure and wanted to throw in the towel! So, I took a week to revise the course and called the Real Estate Commission Approval Board for more clarity. People told me to give up, and my own self-talk was telling me to quit. But my inner voice of perseverance reminded me of the biblical story of David and Goliath. If you're not familiar with the story, David was a small man determined to defeat the giant, Goliath. People said, "David, you can't win. He's much bigger than you, and everyone's afraid of Goliath." David was determined to prove everyone wrong. David went into battle with three stones. The first two stones missed Goliath. Goliath kept getting stronger. I'm sure David felt afraid, tired, defeated, embarrassed, and many other emotions. But our thoughts are the most powerful tools we've got. So, David threw the third stone and Goliath was defeated! On my third real estate course submission, the Real Estate Commission approved my course! As a result, I've taught thousands of students, been recognized locally and internationally for my writings, won numerous awards, and made history by becoming one of the youngest instructors to own a real estate school and the first to write a real estate course on topics others found unpopular and challenging.

Are you aching for greatness? Does your vision seem bigger than you? If so, welcome to

"Perseverance: The Gateway to Triumph."

What is perseverance? According to the Merriam-Webster Dictionary, perseverance is "continued effort to do or achieve something despite difficulties, failure, or opposition; the action or condition or an instance of per-severing; steadfastness."

Perseverance is your gateway to triumph. So often, the pressures and difficulties of life tend to overtake us. Because of the difficulties, we tend to pursue the easy path. But you read my story, and it's time for you to adopt the David and Goliath principles. Wouldn't it be helpful to have some perseverance tools to help guide you throughout life's journey? Let's get started.

Perseverance Principle #1-Start Small

- Despise not small beginnings. It does not matter the size of the tree; it started with a small seed. That small seed produces a big tree. Do you have a seed?

- Your seed has the ability to produce after its own kind but must be watered daily and given positive reinforcement. Then, it will mature and grow.

- Every "somebody" was once a "nobody."

Perseverance Principle #2-Keep Walking on Water

"If we are facing in the right direction, all we have
to do is keep on walking."
—Buddhist saying

- You may not be where you want to be, but you are closer than you were yesterday.

- Trust the direction (tides), even when it seems off course.

- Set your mind such that regardless of what may come, hell or high water, you will persevere.

Perseverance Principle #3-Embrace that Perseverance is Hard Work!

"Perseverance is the hard work you do after you
get tired of doing the hard work you already did."
—Newt Gingrich

- It's easy to quit, make excuses, or join a quitter's club to justify why you shouldn't persevere, but you gain nothing.

- Embrace the fatigue, confusion, despair, lack of sleep, and rejection. It's all part of the process to strengthen your perseverance "muscles."

- You will look back and say, "At the end, this was well worth it."

- If it doesn't cost you, it won't value you.

Perseverance Principle #4-Finish the Course

"The race is not given to the swift, nor the strong, but he who endures until the end."
—Ecclesiastes 9:11

- Growth is better than swelling. Growth will sustain itself, while swelling will eventually burst. Swelling cannot endure for the long term.

- Success requires long-term commitment. It requires you to finish the course. It requires persistence.

- Stop paying attention to time because everything happens in its season.

- Difficult things take a long time, impossible things a little longer.

Apply these principles daily, along with action, and watch your "perseverance muscles" enhance.

In conclusion, create a lifestyle of preserving! Challenge your mind, soul, body, and spirit to get out of their comfort zone. I tell people all the time to never fear failure and instead fear being comfortable. Comfort gives place to ignorance. Perseverance is a requisite for life. You will encounter many situations in which it is required. Your problems show you where you need to improve and what you need to focus on. Thank God for the many obstacles in your life. With enough time, you can accomplish any mountain, swim any deep sea, cross any desert, and make history while helping others achieve theirs as well. Don't give up! Don't give up! You are too close.

Are You Ready to Free Yourself?

Tabatha Carr

I'm free! I'm finally FREE. Are you ready to free yourself and triumph from weight challenges, hormone challenges, fibroids, cysts, lack of energy, blood pressure challenges, and blood sugar challenges? I know how you feel. As I look back at my life before I was FREE, I would ask myself, "Why do I keep sabotaging myself?" I know God hears my prayer. I pray the same prayer all the time. So why am I still fat? I've been over 200 pounds since I was in high school. Why am I still fat? Does this sound like you?

I write this chapter hoping that I can help change your life, and for some, save your life.

I know there are millions of women, maybe including you, going through the same thing I went through—not knowing where to turn or in whom to confide and being left with no hope. Smiling on the outside and crying and self-sabotaging on the inside. I'm here to tell you there is hope. God brought you here to live a full life, and He has extraordinary plans for you.

How many times have you lost weight and gained it right back? Do you start a new diet every New Year? Believe me, I've been there. I've tried countless diets and spent thousands of dollars on food for special recipes, supplements, programs, gyms, exercise gadgets, and books. Don't get me wrong, just like you, I would always lose at least five pounds. Sometimes I would lose 20 pounds. However, the weight always found its way back to my stomach, hips, thighs, and butt. And let's not forget the upper arm flab that seems to get bigger by the year. Then the cycle starts over again the next year. I would ask myself, "How could I not lose one pound? How is that possible? What type of a failure am I for not even being able to lose one pound but gaining another 10?"

I went up to a size 22 in high school. It was during this time that I was prescribed blood pressure pills at the tender age of 16. This is the age when I started seeing the stretch marks all over and started being bullied for being fat. The combination of my weight, stretch marks all over my body, and the fact that I had to take medication drastically lowered my self-esteem and confidence. But I hid it well. No one knew the depression behind the smile. From that point, I felt that I was never enough. We lay the foundation in our early years, and at the time, I didn't understand this concept. I didn't understand that the rest of my life would be shaped based on how I felt about myself. I went on to live a mediocre life of fear and settling instead of going after my dreams.

Every year that went by, I began to develop more and more health problems. I had high blood pressure, high blood sugar, and depression, to name a few. There was one challenge that I wasn't ready for, but it changed my life.

At the age of 35, I was still single, had no children and yes, you guessed it, still fat. Hormone problems hit me hard, and it scared me so badly I didn't know what to do or to whom to turn. I bled for three months non-stop. My mother, grandmother, aunt, and cousin had hysterectomies before they turned 40. The difference between them and me is they all had children and they weren't planning on having anymore. I told God it couldn't be my time. Not yet. I hadn't had kids. Of course, the doctor was saying surgery or more medication. I said no. I prayed and said, "It's just me and You, God." I asked God to heal me. He showed me exactly what my body needed, and the bleeding stopped. This was a turning point for me. I knew that if I didn't make a change, my health would continue to decline. I was battling with weight, blood pressure, blood sugar, heart palpitations, and hormones. What I didn't realize is all of these issues could be fixed by changing my diet. Guess what? It's not about the latest diet fad. It's not about all protein and no carbs. It's not about being paleo or vegan. It's about nutrition and giving your body the food it needs to burn fat and perform optimally. It's about staying active. One thing I had to do was work on my emotions and my self-esteem. I realized I had goals and dreams that I wasn't pursuing because of my weight. I would often stay home instead of engaging with friends. It was about identifying the root cause of why I would overeat and start a diet over and over again. It was about changing my habits. It was about nourishing my gut.

Today, I'm free. Free from high blood pressure. Free from high blood sugar. Free from the threat of a hysterectomy. My choice of having children is back. I woke up on New Year's Day for the first time in my life without a resolution to lose weight.

Going through this, I had no idea what God's plan was. Now I understand why God took me through this. Now, I am a naturopathic doctor specializing in women's health. As women, we have a unique set of nutritional requirements. I educate women, specifically those who are struggling with weight, hormones, a lack of energy, blood sugar, and blood pressure. I want you to know that there is hope, and the life you want is waiting on you. It's time for you to get to a place where you don't wake up another year with the same weight loss resolution.

It's time to break the chains and free yourself. Start by writing out your health goals. Don't rush through this process. Then ask yourself, "How will my life change when I reach this goal?" So many times, we put our life on hold due to our health, but it is at a cost. We will never get back yesterday, so I challenge you today to break this cycle and free yourself. Live the life God has planned for you. Are you ready to get rid of the old life to have the life that is waiting for you?

The number one health sabotage is sugar. Sugar weakens your thyroid, which is responsible for burning fat. A weakened thyroid can also cause hair loss. Sugar weakens your adrenals, which control a hormone called cortisol. Your adrenals are responsible for controlling your stress, which can be physical or emotional, and eating the wrong foods for our body will contribute to stress. Your adrenals also metabolize proteins and carbs, and too much stress can lead to overproduction of cortisol, which will lead to increased belly fat. Too much sugar also feeds the bad bacteria in your gut, which affects your digestion. And if excess glucose is in your blood, it gets stored as fat. Start paying attention to how much sugar is in ketchup, barbeque sauce and spaghetti sauce. Two or three table-spoons of some brands of ketchup and barbeque sauce have the same amount of sugar if not more than a scoop of ice cream. These are items that we sometimes don't think about when we are cutting sugar out of our diet. Too much stress is a major contributing factor to reproductive health problems, and there is a direct correlation between mental and emotional stress and the body's ability to fight or resist an illness.

Get moving. If you want to increase your metabolism, burn more fat, have more energy, and increase your serotonin (which is a natural mood stabilizer), exercise is an absolute must. Low levels of serotonin can cause you to be depressed, which can cause you to overeat if you eat based on your emotional state.

Drink half your body weight in water on a daily basis. Drinking water is often overlooked as a tool for weight loss and good health. Water keeps your pipes clean and the metabolism up. A lack of water causes problems with energy, digestion, elimination, and respiration. If the brain, which is 85 percent water, is dehydrated, it has to get energy from food, which will cause you to crave sugar. Increasing water will reduce sugar cravings and fat deposition.

While addressing your hormones, activity, and water, your digestion also needs to be nourished. A sluggish digestive system will hinder weight loss. Probiotics will help build up the digestive system, and a good food enzyme will help you digest food.

These are simple steps that you can implement immediately. Get to the root of your emotions and hormones, correct your diet, and stop sabotaging yourself! It's your time. You are worth it! It's time to claim the victory and start celebrating your triumph.

The Runway of My Life

Tonia Marie Robinson

GIFT:
TRIUMPH

When you're 21 years old, you're judged "Miss North Valley Phoenix," and the judges drape a Miss North Valley banner on you, it feels a whole lot better than when you're a few years younger and the kids call you "Olive Oil with Skis."

And you think, "Wow, everything's gonna be great now."

And other people think, "Wow, she's got it made."

And they see you on the runway, and you work in the film industry with major, major stars, and you start your own TV show, and people say, "I wouldn't mind looking like her (or going out with her). I'd love to have doors open up for me like that and be given her opportunities. Gimme her life over mine any day."

You know where this is going, right?

You know that what people see on the surface is never what's real on the inside. You know that what it looks like in front of the camera is never what's going on behind the scenes. (And I'm not just talking about all the Hollywood closed-door happenings that are finally coming out in the open.)

You know that people who maybe don't look super glamorous from magazine standards—and especially people who may look like they have strong physical difficulties and disfigurations—are misjudged all the time.

But what most people don't know is that many, many, many of us who are made up for "show" and for show business are also misjudged, misunderstood, and even mistreated.

Let me tell you, it felt a whole lot better to be judged "Miss" something than to be misjudged for something. We wonder whom we can trust and sometimes get it wrong. We can be lied to, betrayed, abused. Treated like meat.

Yes, "Me, too."

And some people—not you, but some people—see us on the runway or in films or on TV and say, "She can't be smart. She's probably kinda stupid. She even gets her words mixed up sometimes, so you really can't take her seriously."

But none of that is what we're going to talk about now. There's no point in getting stuck there. And that's my point.

You see, everybody is misjudged, and everybody misjudges.

Because we don't see beyond the surface, and sometimes we don't show others what's going on behind the scenes.

This year alone, I lost some family members. Nine family members, in fact. Now, having been a hospice nurse and a VA nurse, I knew how to show a brave, smiling face on the outside—eyelash extensions and great new hair and everything—but what I didn't show was how hurt I was on the inside. Literally. My doctors knew, though. The tests showed elevated cancer risk on the inside.

I had to change the trauma to triumph so our family wouldn't lose ten family members. That's what we're going to talk about now.

Let me tell you what I did. And truthfully, what I'm still doing (because this is an ongoing process). And what you can do, too.

First of all, you need to be a diva.

That's right.

You need to be a diva. You need to make friends with your "inner diva" so you can make a real difference in your life and in other people's lives.

Because I'm a diva and proud of it.

Don't you judge me now. Because I'm not an ordinary diva. You see, when people who didn't understand said, "She's a diva." I said, "Hell, yes! I'm a diva, all right. Not only that, I'm a diva with purpose!"

Let me tell you what that is, why you should also be a diva with purpose, and how you can become a diva with purpose.

A diva with purpose is being okay in your own skin.

A diva with purpose is resilience, determination, loyalty.

A diva with purpose is dedicated.

A diva with purpose knows how to be supportive.

A diva with purpose volunteers in the community.

A diva with purpose always empowers and motivates.

And a diva with purpose never betrays.

This is why "Olive Oil with Skis" grew up to form a nonprofit organization called—you guessed it—Divas with Purpose.

Our purpose, our mission, is to embrace uniqueness, celebrate diversity, uplift, empower, unite, support, and provide resources to all women. We discuss topics such as teen suicide, depression, loss, and self-worth.

Tomorrow morning when you wake up and you look in the mirror and you're about to misjudge yourself, STOP.

Say, "Good morning, Diva!"

And get to work fulfilling your purpose.

And tomorrow afternoon when someone misjudges or misunderstands or mistreats you, just think, "They don't know they're dealing with a diva."

And keep on fulfilling your purpose.

And today, join us. We have a lot of work to do, a lot of people to help, and a whole planet to heal.

Not only that, but you get to wear whatever hair you want and rock your very own "Miss Diva with Purpose" banner.

And I'm personally inviting you to join us and support us.

Welcome, Divas with Purpose.

Thongs and Support Hose Don't Go Together!

MY JOURNEY TO TURNING 40

Harriette P. Gibbs

GIFT:
TRIUMPH

That's right, I said it. "Thongs and support hose don't go together." Forty? Oh hell no! Not me! I mean, I feel like I just graduated from college. I still like designer jeans, I like to party, hell, I even like watching cartoons. For what? Forty. Stop it! Stop saying the "F" word. I'm too young to hear the "F" word. Oh, please stop saying it. For God's sake, I'm still 39. Yeah, I said it. Thirty-nine. Now doesn't that sound better? Thirty-nine. Yeah, I like that. It's better than that damn "F" word. Oh, you know the word. Don't sit there and pretend you don't know what I am talking about.

How did this happen? I mean, I was asleep and woke up forty? I mean, did I travel through time and enter into a new dimension? Just what is it? Or could I still be asleep? I actually think my mother gave me the wrong birthdate information; I probably was born in 1975. I remember distinctly turning 30, and I was excited. I remember sweet 16, and then 18, and then wanting to be 21, and then wanting to be 25, and then wanting to be 30. But, I don't remember wanting to be 40. Forty just invited itself in. Forty just came on in just like one of my ghetto family members. You know, the ones who just pop over unannounced and then inform you that they are going to stay a while. Well, that's what 40 did.

This forty thing scared me. All of a sudden, at the age of 39, I felt as though I was about to fall apart. I am a caramel-colored sista who is voluptuous and without any health problems—except for the voluptuous part. However, the doctor calls it obesity. But what does he know? Anyway, I was walking around and dropping it like it was hot, and all of a sudden, I started having back problems. I thought I could simply go to physical therapy as I did in the past and get fixed. Well, this time, I went to physical therapy, and I didn't get fixed. My back problem went from an annoying pain to absolutely excruciating. I was laid out flat from November to February. I couldn't stand. I couldn't sit. All I could do was lie. I was miserable from December to January. I lost 23 pounds. When you feel as I did, the last thing you want to think about is going to the bathroom. I was surrounded by four walls, and I felt as if I was closed off from the world. I wondered why this was happening to me. I felt as though I was a good person, so why me? I cried daily because I didn't know what was happening to me. At times I wanted to die because I just could not imagine living like this. In December, I found out the pain in my back was due to a herniated disc. I lay in the bed and said, "Is this what forty is going to bring me? A broken-down body? If that's the case, keep forty, because forty is not too friendly." All I can say is thank God for surgery. I had back surgery in February, and God brought me through a very scary time. I am able to sit, stand, and walk again. I am thankful to be alive, yet I was still scared of this forty thing. It was like I was just seeing my life slipping away right in front of my eyes. Although none of us know the day or the hour we will leave this planet, it just felt that 40 was putting me closer to leaving this world. So, what would I do? Would I let this forty thing cripple me, or would I embrace it?

My name is Harriette, and I had a choice to make—whether or not I accept my new age. You may say, "Girl, you really don't have a choice in the matter." Yet, I would say I did. I could begin to fight this thing by having an "extreme makeover of my mindset," or I could refuse to grow up. So you see, I did have a choice.

See, in my eyes, at 40, I was supposed to be super sexy. I thought at 40 it was going to be thongs all day. I was in the prime of my life. Yet the doctor told me I needed support hose for those swollen ankles. I had major back surgery. I needed glasses because my eyes were changing, or as my eye doctor stated, "You're at that age." Insert rolls eyes at the doctor! Then I was like "Support hose? Thongs and support hose don't go together." I was crushed. I was like, "Lawd, I really feel like an old person. What's next, a cane? Come on, 40, you gotta do better than this!"

So here I was, facing an age that so many women had said would be the greatest part of my life; an age at which I was really coming into womanhood. In reality, this age had become one of the scariest and toughest times of my life.

I was living, but not really living. I was listening to everyone else tell me what my life was supposed to be like and not defining it for myself. You know, society tends to impose some of their philosophies onto you, and if you're not careful, you began to subscribe to it. In reality, there is no one way to live this thing called life. I'm sure you may have heard things like, "By a certain age, you're supposed to have a good job. At this age, you are supposed to be married, have the big house, and have two kids and a puppy." The list goes on and on. So many damn rules. It was at times like this that I simply wanted to throw in the towel and give up because my life wasn't unfolding in this manner. I had the house and the husband, yet by 48, I became a widow. I wasn't blessed to be the mother that I always wanted to be. I felt out of place because at this age, I still wanted to explore more. I wanted to take a step into the world of entrepreneurship. Again, I was scared because some of society would say that I was too old to explore entrepreneurship and that I should be content in my current career. I was falling deeper and deeper into simply giving it all up.

How do you get past all of this? Is forty really the pits, or is it simply full of wonderful lessons as I really come into myself? Sure, I could have said no to pursuing my dream of becoming an author because of what others may say, but I turned it around and realized that I truly only have one life to live. So, what would I do with this one life God has given me? I choose to live on my own terms and set goals, and I will keep pursuing my entrepreneurial vision. I realize that I have a purpose that only I can pursue. As I went through my forties, it wasn't really all that bad. Of course, it had its challenges, but that's life. No one ever said that life would be easy, and it's not. Yet, it's this beautiful journey that God designed just for me. Even in my darkest hour, God has always proven to be right there with me. Through every crazy and good decision, God has never left my side. God has carried me through every trial and every triumph of forty. I'm excited to see the other "F" words—"Fifty and Fabulous." I feel just that—fabulous.

I accept my inner child and allow her to play at times and create amazing journeys. I finally accept me! Yes, I accept me and all my flaws, all my quirks, all my talents, and all my gifts that were given to me. I realize that I had to come into a season of loving on me, and I rose up like the Phoenix. It was time to stop feeling sorry for myself, put on my big girl thongs, oops, I mean panties, and start doing what I wanted to do. Some of my goals were to become an entrepreneur and become an author. So, I published my first book in 2015, and I'm now the CEO of the Howard and Elizabeth Caldwell Foundation. My motto has always been: "Moving from a dream chaser to a dream catcher." At some point, I had to stop just chasing a dream and really sit down and capture it. Heck, I'm writing a book with the fabulous Kim Coles! Talk about capturing a dream! Dream captured. Just think, if I had given up, you wouldn't be reading this chapter. So, my sister, know that you are beautiful and amazing. You beam with swag, personality, and possibilities. You are never too old to stop going after your dreams. No one can tell you how to live this thing called life. Be fearless and march to the beat of your drum. Life is defined by moments, so enjoy the moments. Be courageous. Do something that you always wanted to do but were afraid to do. Share your creativity and live your God-given purpose. More importantly, live!

Overcoming Insurmountable Odds in the Face of Adversity

Lisa Guerrant, PhD

I slid across the stage, still in awe, star struck for accomplishment; and although the loud cheers and claps encapsulated my eardrums, in my heart, everything was as quiet as a midsummer night's dream. All I could say to myself was, "Wow. I did it. I finally made it!"

How did I get here? How did I ever make it? Have you ever asked yourself these questions? Sometimes in life, we go through trials and tribulations wondering, "How can I survive this?" We often feel that there is no hope and no light at the end of the tunnel. Have you ever felt this way? Did you feel like giving up? These are the exact feelings that tried to rule my life over and over again. I had gone through so much, and it seemed as if that rollercoaster was never going to end; but, this is one time that I am proud to say that I was wrong!

How did I survive the storm and manage my life as a victim of abuse, a teenage mother, a single parent, and an ex-wife? How did I obtain four degrees, including a PhD, and become an author, entrepreneur, master herbalist, and so much more? I still ask myself sometimes, "How is this possible?" It feels so surreal. I used to feel like I was cursed, if there is such a thing. Do you know what that feels like? Have you ever heard the saying "Bad things happen to good people"? Do you equate that saying with your own life? All too often, we accept this particular saying as truth, when in reality, it is a myth; bad things can happen to anyone. I have experienced a lot of adversity in my life. There have been times when I wanted to give up on me, on life, on everything. You see, so often we get wrapped up in our own feelings, and we drown in them. We forget or overlook the fact that we can choose to stay the victim of our circumstance or to be the victor in the battle.

I thought it all started with my first marriage, but I later realized that the feelings I had been harboring were born long before him. My feelings were like a forgotten dinosaur egg that hatched when the world thought dinosaurs were extinct. All the things that hurt me as a young child, I worked hard to exclude from my life. It turns out that those were the very things that kept coming back to haunt me, blindside me, and even though I thought I was in control, they were really controlling me. I allowed myself to fall victim not only to circumstance, but to youthful ignorance and desires. Have you ever experienced that? Do you give so much of yourself that you lose yourself? I did.

By the time I reached the young age of 14, I had been molested on two separate occasions and raped once. My spirit was broken. I could not understand why these things happened to me. Still, through all of this, I remained an A-B student, excelling academically and athletically. School and sports became my safe haven. Unfortunately, that safe haven was taken from me when my coach raped me. I was devastated. I kept quiet. I just couldn't go through another traumatic experience only to have yet another man let off the hook for stealing my very essence. I just knew that if I could get past this, I could lock it all away and live my life in peace. A few months passed, and I had locked all of my feelings away in Pandora's box. That all changed one cold day in October 1988 when I heard three life changing words: "You are pregnant." I could hear the whispers as I walked by. "Well, she will definitely be a drop out!" "Poor thing, her life is over." I remember saying to myself, as my eyes filled with tears, "Why are they saying these things about me?" It was such a horrible feeling and a nightmare of a reality that I had to confront, whether I wanted to or not. Unfortunately, the baby was not blessed with life. Although I was hurt beyond recognition, somehow, this had to be a sign that I was going to be blessed with the gift of new life. There was no way that the path I had left to travel was going to bring any more trauma. I was wrong.

The next year I found myself pregnant, not by rape, but by love. How did this happen? I was being so careful. As much as I kept questioning this, it really did not matter to me. As mothers, we are bound by unsaid sacred rules of protection, and I knew I had to protect my precious little baby. Again, the stares and whispers were damaging to my soul. The words they spoke haunted me. How could anyone say such horrible things about me? I didn't know what to do. But, through it all, my mother stood by my side just as she always had. She loved me, nurtured me, and helped me carry the burdens of the world that were upon me. For once, I felt strong.

In October 1989, I had a beautiful, healthy baby girl. She changed my life. She was all that I lived for. She made the juggling of parenthood and high school worth every sacrifice. Due to unforeseen daycare issues, I had to choose between continuing school and taking care of my child. I chose her! I withdrew from school, signed up to take the GED, and immediately enrolled in junior college. Shortly thereafter, I was married. In a matter of months, I had become a mother, a wife, and a college student. Life was great. My saga was over, or so I thought. Life and love proved me wrong. Four children and six years later, love failed. I was divorced. I was exhausted and depressed, but I knew that I could not give up. That was not the message that I wanted my four beautiful children to receive. That was not the legacy I wanted to leave behind. I chose to be the victor! I chose to fight the odds and show the world that I was and am the queen that God created me to be.

Life was a struggle, but every moment was worth it as long as I knew my children were safe and loved unconditionally. I did everything I could to keep the light lit at the end of the tunnel, and then one day, the sun was shining brighter than it ever had before. Love found me. Surely there is no way that this could be taken away from me. Yet again, I was wrong. Distrust and infidelities riddled my life, crumbling my soul. Crumbling the very essence of a woman that existed in me. I wanted to die. Do you know what that feels like? I gave up. Just as I imagined leaving this realm, my life flashed in front of me as if I was in a time travel. I saw the faces of my children and my grandchildren. I saw them hugging me and loving me, and this gave me new life. Life was not over; life was just beginning.

The road I had traveled, although riddled with pain and suffering, made me strong. It made me strong enough to bear the weight of the world to protect my children; to continue to go to school; to be the victor and not the victim. Here I am now—a mother of four, a grandmother of seven, living and loving life as Dr. Lisa Guerrant. I am proud to be who I am. Oftentimes, we are knocked down, and instead of jumping right back up, we allow our feelings or our immediate responses to control our thoughts. I will admit that it is human nature to follow those steps, but when we are seeking greatness, when we are stretching our arms to reach heights beyond the mountaintop, we are sometimes challenged to see if we are worthy of the blessings that are coming our way. Are you strong enough to handle the good with the bad? The highs and the lows? Everything happens for a reason. The objective is to use these mysterious events as building blocks and stepping stones to stay on your path. Everything you experience in life is shaping you for the future and giving you the tools to be able to throw other stones, or even boulders, out of your way as you continue onward with your journey. Life is not perfect. It is not designed with the intent to make things easy. But, it is designed with the intent to teach you, strengthen you, and most importantly, help you grow spiritually, mentally, emotionally, and physically as you get to know "you."

In stillness, you will find your true self! Be great. Be true. Be you!

Shattered into Purpose

Wendy Shurelds

GIFT:
TRIUMPH

I believe that no matter what you go through, whether it's tragedy or a life-threatening disease, you can turn it into a positive by making an impact

I certainly don't look like all that I've endured. I've had so much tragedy in my life—losing my mom, dad, and close friend and fighting for my own life. I have allowed my journey and all that I've endured to strengthen me to help others. What God has placed in me is the desire to inspire.

What does a nightmare look like to you? A nightmare to me is like someone snatching you up like a thief in the night, sucking the life out of you.

Early 2008 is when my nightmare snatched me up with a phone call informing me my mom was in a preventable work-related incident, which resulted in her death from internal decapitation. Losing my mother in such a horrific manner was devastating and took me over the edge into the dark side in a state of deep depression. I was like a zombie trying to exist as I struggled to move forward. I remained depressed, stressed, and lost for over two years due to not having closure of how my mother died and constantly being woken in the middle of the night. Depression took over my life. I lay in bed day in and day out feeling numb to all that was around me, absorbed and stuck in a dark, unfamiliar place. Have you ever felt stuck in an unfamiliar place? If so, I know you can relate.

It was near the end of 2010 when I finally woke up from the dark side wanting to seek and gain knowledge of how my mother died. I didn't want my mom's death to be in vain, which led me to United Support and Memorial for Workplace Fatalities (USMWF), where I became an activist. I spoke to senators, fought for workers' safety, and allowed my mother's voice to be heard. I didn't want other families to endure a tragedy like mine. Along with USMWF, I helped write the Family Bill of Rights, which was adapted by the Occupational Safety and Health Administration (OSHA). Safety should be employers' number one priority.

I soon realized the power of healing when I set out to fight, make a difference in workplace safety, and provide much needed support and guidance to other families who had lost their loved ones on the job. This work was truly rewarding to my heart. I believe God provides you with the ability to do what is necessary during your most trying times.

In mid-2013, tragedy slid under my door without wiping its feet on the doormat. I was diagnosed with breast cancer and had to fight for my own life. After hearing the big C word, it took time to accept that I had this dreadful, monstrous disease. I was scared, frightened of the unknown, and I really didn't know how to process all the mixed emotions I was currently feeling. I believe the spirit of God lives within us, and I began tapping into my innermost positive spirit, keeping still so I could hear the spirit of God speak to me. I took time for myself to meditate. I talked with God to give me the calming spirit and confirmation I needed to fight and defeat this ugly disease inside my body. I believe your greatness is within your strength to overcome.

I battled breast cancer with a good friend. We were each other's support. We took each other to and from doctor's appointments and surgeries and worked out together. Nobody understands your journey or battle better than a person who has been through or is going through the same thing. Unfortunately, in October 2014, my friend lost her battle and died. I lived, leaving me with survivor's guilt and questions that only God Himself could answer. Yet, I'm still not understanding what God already knows. My friend's death shook me to my core. Once again, I was left devastated, searching from within, and asking God what He needed from me. Have you ever been in a similar situation asking God the same question?

My friend taught and showed me what faith and strength looked like, as she knew she was going to die, accepting death as part of her journey. So many of us have in our mind and heart that God will somehow, someway carry us through to live without ever thinking death is a part of His journey He has chosen for us.

Upon my friend's death, I made her a promise that I would honor her life and share her journey by making others aware of how deadly breast cancer can be. However, at that moment in time, I didn't know how I was going to fulfill my promise.

In November 2014, I formed a team called "Sistahs of Strength" with Susan G. Komen San Diego Race for the Cure in honor of my good friend. During the fundraiser, I won a free airline ticket that led me into the office of Komen San Diego where I met the President and CEO. I told her about my friend and our breast cancer journey, and she told me about the Circle of Promise, which is an African American initiative. She said I should consider getting involved, if not for me then for my good friend. At that time, I felt as though I had a lot on my plate and didn't have time to add anything else. I shared my Komen San Diego office experience with my dad and stated to him that I didn't have time. He told me to make time because this was important, I could make a difference, and this was what I was supposed to do because this was my purpose. Are you saying, "Wow," because I sure did!

In 2015, tragedy rung my door bell without saying hello or asking to come in. My world once again came crashing down with the unexpected death of my dad, who was my best friend, confidant, business partner, and just an awesome dad. The unbearable pain I felt was surreal; my heart shattered. Emptiness plagued most of my days after burying my dad. I felt like Job in the Bible, saying, "What else can happen? I've lost everything." But my mind said, "You're not new to this." Can you relate to feeling as though you've lost everything?

During my battle with breast cancer, my dad was one of my biggest cheerleaders besides my daughter, my son, and my fiancé. He gave his time unselfishly as he made sure I had everything I needed, from healthy meals, to financial support, to spiritual advice. I clung to him for dear life because he was my only living parent. I fought like hell to keep my dad alive by putting my own health at risk, as I didn't have a choice or say in my mother's sudden untimely death because her life was taken so tragically. I realize I was being selfish by not wanting him to leave me. Have you ever been selfish by not wanting your loved one to leave you? Or felt that you were all alone? That's how I was feeling.

I believe God places you where He wants you to be, not where you want to be. Also, I believe God has an assignment for your life, and it's up to you to accept it or not. I've accepted my full assignment, which is helping save lives. I never would have imagined the platforms God has created for me. I never asked nor sought anything. It all came to me as if God Himself hand-delivered it. I know you all are dying to know what those platforms are. Drum roll, please. I'm a Community Resource Advocate for Komen San Diego Circle of Promise, advocating on behalf of all women, specifically African American, educating and empowering them to make their breast health a priority by getting their annual mammograms. I go into communities offering free mammograms to those who can't afford them. I'm the host of the Many Shades of Pink & Black Health Radio Talk program, along with Dr. Suzanne Afflalo, on kblkradio.com every Sunday at 2 p.m. PST. Dr. Afflalo and I are the co-founders of Good Health = Long Life—a free community health outreach event that takes place every third Wednesday of each month in the Big Lots parking lot at 1655 Euclid Ave., San Diego, CA., 92105, from 10 a.m. to 6 p.m.

"Make up your mind that no matter what comes your way, no matter how difficult, no matter how unfair, you will do more than simply survive. You will thrive in spite of it."
—Joel Osteen

Self-Love

The Evils of Comparison and the Joy of Self-Love

Bonita Owens

I started on a journey of helping women find their significance because I was that woman who felt that something was missing. I lost my significance. I was disconnected from the essence of me. I completely abandoned the woman that I was and the one that I had the potential to become. Some days, I didn't know if I even liked the person that I saw in the mirror, and I often found myself wishing that I could be someone other than who I was. I just wished that the parts of me that I didn't like were different. The more that I focused on what I wanted to change, the more I missed out on contentment and the joy of being me.

I traced my ill content back to junior high school. There I was, standing on the lawn of one of the most prestigious schools in Tennessee. Although I went to that school because I had excelled academically and I needed a challenge, I wasn't sure if I was supposed to be there. I wasn't sure if I belonged. Have you ever felt as if you didn't quite belong? Before that time, I was pretty confident and self-assured. I received much love and support from my family, I was confident in my abilities, and I thought that I was pretty special. Yep, I thought that I had it going on! Over time, I started to notice how different I was from everyone else. That difference was not to be respected or just acknowledged, but it became a measuring stick which I used to gauge my own self-worth. In other words, I started looking at other people's grass in order to decide how green mine was.

As I interacted with my classmates from affluent backgrounds, I started to focus on what they had that I didn't. They had beautiful homes. I didn't. They had two-parent households. I didn't. They went on nice vacations. I didn't. That's when I started to feel it—I'm not good enough. Not rich enough, not perfect enough, not successful enough.

I wished that I could say that it started and stopped in junior high school. This feeling of not being good enough followed me all the way to adulthood. I wished that I could speak like her, dress like her, decorate like her. I wish that I had a family like hers and a life like hers. The list goes on. When I looked at myself, I simply saw inadequacies, gaps, and shortcomings. Any positive thoughts that I attempted to give myself were quickly swept away with "But I could have done this better."

My confidence waned, although I kept it together pretty well. I wore a pretty nice mask and expressed my pain through judgments and critiques of the people around me. I could at least make myself feel better by finding other people whose lives were worse than mine or who at least had something that I could pick apart and criticize.

All of these issues represented a lack of self-love and self-acceptance. My life became one that was about how I measured up compared to others around me. I seemed so frazzled, fragmented, and imperfect. I only showed up to tell myself what I was doing wrong and what everyone else around me was doing right. I always felt as if I was the only one with a "not so perfect life." I felt that everyone around me had it so much better than I did. Have you ever just felt like you are all by yourself? Trapped in thoughts of feeling inadequate? Have you ever felt that things seem to go right for people around you, but you seem to miss the triumph train by like two minutes?

As my responsibilities grew with my husband, my children, and my career, I would go to bed every night thinking about what I didn't make happen that day or what I should have or could have done. I gave myself a constant tongue lashing. "Bonita, why can't you get it together? What is wrong with you?" I began to think that I was the only one who wasn't organized or who had trouble doing things that I knew were good for me.

Everyone around me seemed to do it better and make it happen. They were better wives, better parents, better daughters, better neighbors. Everyone was better than I was. I had 101 ways that I didn't measure up. This caused stress, anxiety, and emptiness.

It was in 2014 that I discovered why I was so unhappy, stressed, and unfulfilled. For the first time, I was able to name my problem. I did not love myself. The concept of loving myself in the first place was a controversial one for me. I grew up in a religious environment in which the concept of self-love insinuated selfishness or arrogance. The lesson that I learned and experienced was that true service meant suffering and "doing without." I saw this manifest with women in my family. I never celebrated myself. I only looked at what was lacking. For example, I would say things like, "I lost 10 pounds, but it took me a long time to do it."

I forgot to celebrate and appreciate me. What was good about me? What was great about me? What did I love about me? These questions were often difficult and are still difficult at times. Self-love is not promoted much. The Bible says, "love your neighbor as yourself" (Mark 12:31, NIV). The assumption is that you love yourself, but that is an assumption that is not realized by many.

I realized that my relationship with me was a reflection of my relationship with others. I realized that if God loves me, then who am I not to love me? I was treating myself in ways that I would never treat a friend. Self-love means that you get to respect, talk to, and think of yourself like you would a special friend. If a friend was in trouble and struggling, would you lift her up or tear her down? Would you be graceful and patient or would you be unforgiving and critical? What would you say to her? That revelation changed my life. I looked at myself in the mirror one day and said two things: "YOU ROCK!" and "I will never leave you or abandon you again." I made the woman in the mirror a promise. I promised her that she deserved to have a friend who would be in her corner and who would love her unconditionally. I told her that her imperfections were also perfect. I accepted the good and the "not so good," and it is all good!

Ever since I made that declaration, my life has changed. I now go to bed focusing on what I did well and what I would like to do better tomorrow. I no longer compare myself to others to determine where I fit, but I acknowledge the uniqueness in my journey. I can admire a skill or talent in others and still admire the skills and talents within me. Self-love is a birthright. Since God loves us and He created us, we don't have the right to think any less of His creation than He does. As Shakespeare's Hamlet said, "To thine own self be true."

Now I consciously celebrate myself, and I have learned to be satisfied with the woman that I am and the one that I am becoming. My life is more enjoyable, and the stress is gone! I am free to love my family and others as I love myself. I can tolerate others' faults as I tolerate my own. My life is filled with more compassion and less judgment. There is a joy and a freedom that comes with self-love and self-acceptance. It is also a journey that I continue to travel as I help other women find their place of self-love and value. I realized that I am amazing, and you are amazing too!

Now if you are dealing with these issues, I want to invite you to practice the following:

1. Write down five things that you love about yourself.
2. Write down three things that you do well.
3. When you find yourself thinking a critical or harsh thought about yourself, immediately speak to yourself as you would a friend.
4. Speak daily affirmations of self-love.
5. Love yourself by taking care of you. Make time for your mind, body, and spirit.

Love Thyself, First!

Dr. Mia Cowan

Thirty dollars, sixty dollars, ninety dollars. That's how much I collect from my patients in no-show fees daily. It has become a part of our culture for women to always put everyone else's needs before our own.

Dr. Mia: Why did you miss your appointment, Mrs. Smith?

The Mrs. Smiths: I had to take my parents to the doctor; I had to adjust my schedule because my husband forgot about his appointment, so I had to take the kids; My mom was admitted to the hospital; I had a sick kid; I couldn't get off work; the list goes on and on!

Rarely do my patients put themselves before their children, husbands, and families because, as women, we were taught that our happiness should be on the bottom of our priorities. Well, I beg to differ! I watched my mom wake up early to take care of her bed-ridden mother, clean the house, wash clothes, get us ready for school, cook breakfast, take us to school, go to work, go to the grocery store, clean the entire house (with our help when we were old enough), cook dinner, put my daddy's plate on the table, make multiple meals to please the different taste preferences in my household, and never sit down to eat because she may need to pass us something or get us something that she forgot to put on the table. I listened to my dad complain when things were not just right, and I watched him rest after a long day at work while my mother ran around to do everything for everyone else. Therefore, I have no problems with admitting that my happiness is just as important, if not more important, than that of my loved ones. I have yet to see the benefit of putting my happiness after everyone else's. I am willing to take the heat from others, and I am okay with being called "selfish." I watched my mother be an example of the most "unselfish" woman I know, and I am not convinced that it made her life better.

From the time I can remember, certain desires were placed on my heart, and I have tried to live my purpose through my passions without guilt or explanation. I never thought that my parents', my sister's, my aunts' and uncles', my best friends', my children's nor my husband's needs should come before my needs, my happiness, or my fulfilling my God-given purpose on Earth. I have understood for a long time that to maintain my sanity and happiness, I must exercise, get adequate sleep, see my therapist regularly, take the appropriate supplements, herbs and medications, and eat a healthy diet, which all allow me to live my life with passion and purpose. I understand that my spiritual, mental, and emotional health should be more important to me than anyone else's. When my patients miss their appointments, skip mammograms and pap smears, gain weight, avoid exercise, or miss therapy appointments, they don't realize the negative impact these decisions have on their total health and wellness. It breaks my heart to tell someone that they have advanced breast cancer because they did not take the hour out of their year to have a mammogram. It also saddens me to tell someone they have diabetes or endometrial cancer because they did not prioritize their own needs, like exercising or eating healthy to maintain a healthy weight. I spend a lot of my time explaining the importance of prevention, wellness, supplements, exercise, a healthy diet, and hormone balance to my patients, friends, and family. My goal is to teach women that we can have it all! We can be happy and healthy and great mothers, wives, friends, and professionals. However, we must strive to live a life of harmony. Undoubtedly, this will require saying no sometimes, being selfish, and even putting ourselves and our own well-being above everyone else's. And though "total balance" may not be achieved by many, harmony can be achieved by all! To live a life of harmony, we need to focus on optimizing our mental, spiritual, emotional, and physical health, which requires hard work and sacrifice.

I have the pleasure of working with women of all ages. As a result, I have witnessed first-hand the different stages of life. I have also had the pleasure of watching many of my patients age gracefully. As we mature and age, many women begin to notice fatigue and difficulty sleeping, and as a result, more irritability and decreased focus and concentration. At this point in life, usually the 30s and 40s for many women, we are in the prime of our careers, and our children are growing up and becoming more involved. Coincidentally, these are very impressionable years for our children. They watch everything we do and say, and yes, they copy. In essence, if we are tired, miserable, irritable, and not sleeping, we may be teaching our children bad behaviors; remember, they do what we do, not what we say! Our health must be taken seriously because without our health, it is difficult for us to be patient and loving parents, thrive in our careers, or be good wives, daughters, and friends. Though total balance may be a continual work in progress, we can create healthy harmony by doing our part.

As we age, our bodies change significantly. With hormone imbalance, many women can experience weight gain, fatigue, depression, anxiety, insomnia, night sweats, hot flashes, decreased sex drive and orgasms, joint pain, belly fat, and difficulty focusing. When you see your gynecologist or primary care doctor, you can have your levels checked so that you can treat yourself appropriately. With hormonal balance, prevention, exercise, and healthy living, we can all age gracefully and live in harmony.

To live in harmony, we must integrate healthy living into our lives. It is necessary to eat healthy, monitor our weight, and count calories. To age with grace, we must exercise regularly—at least four to six hours per week—incorporating cardiovascular training and resistance training. As we age, we lose muscle, which results in slower metabolism. In turn, this leads to an easy path to undesirable weight gain. Once we become overweight or obese, many chronic diseases will surface. These include hypertension, diabetes, joint pain, back pain, gall bladder disease, heart disease, and many cancers. Therefore, it is necessary to see your physicians for prevention and screening. We must also improve our diets and prepare foods at home instead of eating fast food for convenience. We must increase our intake of fruits and vegetables and lean protein. I do understand as a busy mother and entrepreneur that it is difficult to fit all of this into our already packed day. However, I have learned that I must make my health a priority. So, we must sacrifice to do whatever is necessary to eat right and exercise. If not, we will make the sacrifice later with multiple doctor visits and taking multiple medications in order to treat chronic and preventable diseases. Our health and wellness must become non-negotiable. As such, you may have to pay a trainer, get help preparing your healthy meals at home, wake up earlier, or go to bed later. The bottom line is we must invest time, money, and energy in our health. It is more selfish to ignore your health than to take away time from your family to improve your health. In the long run, if we are sick and can't take care of ourselves, we can become a burden to our families. So, Ageless Belles, it is okay to say no. More importantly, it is okay to love your-self enough to invest in your health and wellness. In this way, you can experience your beauty, balance, and belief to always live well and age beautifully. Love thyself first and live in harmony!

The Path to Self-Love

Chantelle Cotton

Have you ever been on a search for something that you heard existed, but you weren't quite sure of the meaning? I mean, being fully aware that this concept was out there for others to feel and experience but that seemed somehow elusive to you? Well, I have. I have spent the majority of my life on a journey to find and figure out what the word self-love actually meant. Christine Arylo described self-love as "The unconditional love and respect that you have for yourself that is so unwavering that you choose only situations and relationships -- including the one you have with yourself -- that reflect that same unconditional love and respect." This is one of the best descriptions that I have ever found. But even after discovering what the word meant, I still didn't know how to apply it to my own life.

As a young girl, I was very curious but shy at the same time. With my tiny frame and two puffball ponytails,

I was always asking questions and usually getting the wrong answers. As a result of me being misinformed, I made some unfortunate decisions during my teen years. Two of those decisions landed me pregnant at the early age of 15 and again at 16. Can you imagine being a 15-year-old and learning that the stories you had been told about the way the female body worked weren't right at all. And now, as a result, you are pregnant? Talk about devastated!

I did beat all of the odds and went against the stereotypes about young black teens in America, such as "You will never finish high school. You will end up having multiple babies, be on welfare, and living in the projects for the rest of your life."

I actually did graduate high school with my graduating class and went on to be the first person in my family to finish my bachelor's degree and my master's degree. I am so proud to say that with the help of my family, both of my children have obtained their own bachelor's degrees too. I have excelled at every one of my jobs and been one of the top sales producers at every company where I have worked. I worked my way up the corporate ladder and eventually transitioned into entrepreneurship. So, I would say that what may have been intended for my demise, God turned around for my good.

I must admit, for a long time if you looked at me from the outside, you would see that although I accomplished a lot and beat the odds, I still was not a whole person on the inside. I had no idea who I was, and I harbored a lot of resentment, anger, pain and unforgiveness. As a result of this identity crisis, I allowed a lot of negativity into my life. I was a "victim" and kept asking, "Why me?" Why did I have to be the one who got pregnant after only having intercourse two times in my life? Why did I have to be the one not to learn my lesson the first time? Why wasn't communication a common thing in my household? I wore the veils of "why" and "shame" for a very long time. I was broken and so confused that I would accept any type of relationship or friendship into my life. I didn't think I was worthy of anything more. Why would a good guy want me? Why would a girl want to be my friend? I was already tarnished, or so I thought, therefore I accepted treatments and behaviors that were not good for me or to me. I endured a lot of mental, emotional, and physical abuse. I had no idea that I didn't have to allow those things into my life, but I also didn't think that I deserved anything better. I had no idea how to be a friend to anyone or in relationship with anyone because I wasn't even a friend to myself.

Until one day while in college and in yet another toxic relationship. In a heated argument, my boyfriend asked me a question that literally changed the course of my life. "How do you expect for me to love you when you don't even love yourself?" I was astonished, and my first response was, "What do you mean I don't love myself? Of course I love myself!" His response to me was "No, you don't!" and he walked out the door. From that day forth, I was on a quest to figure out what "loving myself" actually meant.

It has been a long road of self-discovery and acknowledgement to get to the point where I am today—fully loving the me I see when looking into a mirror. The more I learned about myself, my likes and my dislikes, the more I learned to forgive myself from the past. All of that heaviness that I used to carry began to fall away. I created a process that helped me to learn to believe in myself from the inside out. I looked up everything in the Bible that God said about me, and I would repeat them in the mirror over and over again until I believed them. Two of my favorites are: "I am fearfully and wonderfully made" (Psalm 139:14, NIV) and "'For I know the plans I have for you,' declares the Lord" (Jeremiah 29:11, NIV). I read self-help books and surrounded myself with positive people and things. The more I started to believe those scriptures and affirmations, the more confident I became. As time passed, I no longer allowed people who weren't adding value to be in my life. I stopped being in toxic relationships and learned how to be a good friend to others. Therefore, my relationships changed and became healthy. My search for love in all the wrong places diminished the more I found the love in myself.

I went from a victim to a victor. For this, I have to thank my dad, who is no longer with us in this world. It wasn't until my father's passing that I realized that not knowing how to love myself was the reason my one desire had not yet been fulfilled.

My father knew that in order for me to ever be united with a man who would honor and cherish me as I deserved, I would first have to know that I deserved it and treat myself in the same manner. I showed my daddy that I could finish high school, complete college, get a post-graduate degree, succeed in a six-figure job, have healthy friendships, be responsible, and take care of my kids. But I never showed him that I could choose the right man for me. Because he is no longer with us, he will not have the opportunity to witness that or walk me down the aisle when I meet the man God tailor-made just for me. But I know he will be there in the spirit.

When you love yourself, you don't allow people to put their hands on you or emotionally abuse you. You know that you're worth more, and it's easy to walk away. Just like I created a process for learning to love myself, I created a process for what I need in a loving, healthy relationship with a man. I call it "The 5 C's." The first C is Christ. Christ is the head of my life, and I need a partner who believes in God so that we can pray together and separately. The second C is communication. In order to have a healthy relationship, you must have strong communication skills, which include listening to understand and not just to respond. The third C is compatibility. If you communicate enough, through fact finding, spending time together, and discovery you should be able to determine if you are compatible or not. If you are utilizing the first two C's, that shouldn't be hard to figure out. The fourth C is consistency. If you are consistent in the first three C's, then you can achieve the fifth C, which is commitment. Since I desire a relationship that is monogamous and can lead to marriage, this is something that I look for when engaging with a potential mate. If you are communicating and spending time together, then eventually, the intentions of the person in the relationship will be revealed, and you will know if this is something you should continue to pursue or not. When a relationship is going in the right direction and is at least meeting these five C's, then I know my father will be smiling down on me from Heaven saying, "Now, my dear child, I can rest."

Fear Is Expensive

JOURNEY TO LOVING MYSELF

Che Haughton

GIFT:
SELF-LOVE

What is self-love? Of course, I knew the formal definition; but, in my mind, self-love was defined as someone showing interest in me, saying "I love you" with little to no action, making enough money to live comfortably, or achieving goals that were set before me. I am sure some can relate. I did not learn or fully understand what self-love was until my adult life. This was a life lesson that I learned the hard way. One day, I woke up at 30 years old a borderline diabetic, morbidly obese at 325 pounds, with high blood pressure, a newborn daughter, no one to tell me that they loved me, no self-control, no ambition, and no motivation. It took the next seven years to learn how crucial loving oneself is to living your best life.

When you are at the lowest point in your life, it is hard to see the top. Fear is expensive. I was accustomed to life being the way that it was for many years. Fear cost me many years of my life! So where do you start? This is how I overcame obesity, fell in love with myself, and started living my best life.

Let's go back to as long ago as I can remember. I've always been overweight. I am sure that I weighed close to 400 pounds in high school. I was made fun of and laughed at and was the butt of most jokes. It was the most debilitating and humiliating experience of my life. It still shakes my core when I think about it. Being a fatherless child, I looked for love in all the wrong places. Into my adult life, I was always the smart one, a career-driven money maker, but I never had a "real boyfriend." I only met men online because I could be whoever I wanted to be and never had to meet them. This all caused me to overeat and love on something that wouldn't make fun of me or judge—food! It was always there, always satisfying, always forgiving, and never judged.

Fast forward to 2010. I became a new parent to a little girl. I weighed 325 pounds. I was sad, depressed, unmotivated, heartbroken, alone, and lost. High blood pressure, diabetes, arthritis, and joint pain were all a part of my everyday life. How could I care for my daughter emotionally, mentally or physically in this condition? Self-love was something I had to do for us! It took me 2,555 days (seven years) to beat this addiction and take my life back. Yes, it was an addiction. Addiction is defined as "the fact or condition of being addicted to a particular substance, thing, or activity."

How did I beat my food addiction?

In our community, we believe that counseling is a waste of time or that it is not helpful. This is where my journey began.

MENTAL HEALTH

I went to talk to someone who did not know me. She only knew that I was depressed based on the way that I looked (yes, depression shows on the outside), the way I carried myself (head hanging down and no eye contact), and the tears that I shed when she introduced herself. This took courage. I did not go there with any expectations because of what society tell us. However, I will never forget that first exercise. Write down everything and everyone that you feel has wronged you and why you feel they have wronged you. I started with my father because as a young woman with no father figure, I became more dependent on things that could show me "love." After I wrote down these things, the counselor had me burn the list. Ashes to ashes, dust to dust. It was gone. I felt the weight being lifted just from pouring out all of those feelings. Meditation also played a major role. It helped me to find my center. By finding my center, I focused more on peace and patience than on pacifying emotions with food.

FORGIVENESS

During counseling sessions, I learned to forgive myself. That was so important. How could I forgive anyone else? I forgave myself for all of the past mistakes and all of the hurt I had been harboring. Then I forgave those whom I felt wronged me. This started with me picking up the phone and calling my estranged father after years of not being on the best terms. He answered. We talked. I apologized. (I didn't wait for him to apologize to me.) He thanked me. "I didn't have the courage to do it, so thank you for reaching out," he said. Two years later, he died. What if I hadn't reached out? I would have continued to carry that hurt. This is where my breakthrough progressed!

THE STRUGGLE

Anything worth having is worth working for, right? Absolutely, but there was struggle. Lots of struggle! Struggle to find my smile again. Where did it go? Struggle with myself over food choices, not wanting to go work out, choosing others over me, fighting with my old self, preventing my new self from being born. It took time to break those bad habits. It will not happen overnight. I did not gain weight overnight, so I had to come to the realization that it wouldn't be lost overnight. Get real with yourself. You may fall down, but get back up. When I became the most important thing to me, I realized that the struggle was not that big. We spend hours at our jobs and in relationships and friendships but fail to spend those same hours on being the best versions of ourselves. Place yourself first!

Train Your Thoughts

Training my thoughts was the most difficult part of this journey because I had to get real with myself. My thoughts would always lean toward the negative, from "No one will ever love me" to "I will fail as a mother." Each time I felt my thoughts going in a negative direction, I would insert a power word. "I will *not* fail. I *will* lose weight. I *can* do this! I *do not* need that extra slice of pizza. Are you really hungry? Or are you attempting to mask something?" These are all of the hard questions that I had to ask myself. Please do not skip this step. Oftentimes, we are lying to ourselves. A breakthrough will not happen until you start to correct yourself.

Finding My Worth

Why was my job, relationship, and family more important than my temple? Something that God granted me the privilege of having and taking care of. It was not until I became the most important thing to me that I knew just how much I was worth!

I avoided mirrors. I only saw my imperfections. I refused to take pictures. My beauty was found by facing myself in the mirror. That seems so simple, but it was the most difficult task. Until one day, I looked in the mirror and saw dimples. I had to learn to love myself when I was 325 pounds. I love myself enough to eat the best foods (I am currently pescatarian), to work out (three to five days per week), control my thoughts, place myself first, and love myself more than anyone else could. I fell in love with myself—my wide-set eyes, newfound dimples, gap teeth, and all. It all makes me who I am. Me! And I am worthy! I found my smile.

Doing this work afforded me complete control of my life. Today, I stand here having lost 160 pounds and understanding my worth, even if it comes from me alone. Be brave enough to face your fears, demand respect, and fall in love with taking care of yourself—mind, body, and spirit. You are capable of living your best life! Do the work so you can smile again too!

"You have to love yourself because no amount of love from others is sufficient to fill the yearning that your soul requires from you."
—Dodinsky

My Journey Back to Me

Dr. Christi Monk

Every little girl envisions the day when she will grow up and have this perfect life—a man who adores the ground she walks on, a nice big house, a fancy car, a maid, and lots of money. I shared my desire to be married with my pastor. His words will forever be etched in my memory. "Have you ever thought about counseling?" If you are like me, you are thinking, "That's an odd question." With a puzzled response and frowned face, I answered, "No." Basically he was saying I needed to be the best person I could be to myself before I entered into any type of relationship; this includes friendships, marriages, partnerships, or any type of relationship in which your actions will have a direct impact on someone else. Okay, I guess that made sense. I was already the best single I could be, or so I thought. I trusted my pastor, so I decided to give counseling a try. In 2010, my life was forever improved because of spiritual counseling.

When I went to my first session, I did not know what to expect. I thought about what I had seen on television. I envisioned candles burning, dimmed lights, a kneeling altar, and a bowl for cleansing. You know, something like a séance. Oh, how wrong was I.

The first session was interesting. Before I was comfortably seated, the first thing out of my counselor's mouth was, "Your feminine side was never nurtured." Huh? What? In hindsight it was true, but she did not know me like that.

The initial task in the first session was to complete a quite lengthy, detailed personality test. As with most personality tests, it was spot on, at least for that season of my life. As part of the 12-week process, we used the book *In Search of Significance* as the foundation for my healing. We started with the meaning of my name which is "follower of Christ." How ironic was that?

Contrary to what I expected from that first visit, it was a very pleasant experience, and I couldn't wait for my next session. Actually, I looked forward to them all. Clarity is cleansing, especially when God is leading it. The spiritual cleansing process forced me to take a deeper look into the actions and decisions that I made in life that negatively impacted who God had created me to be.

I am the oldest girl, but the second child. As the oldest girl, I had the greatest responsibility of my siblings. It was an honor, of course—at first. As I became an adult, I learned not to cry or show emotion. I knew I had to get things done. I learned to lead others. Think for others.

Tell others what to do and how to do it. This is when I learned how to be controlling. I was in control of everything. Which resulted in my dominating my relationships with men, which is another story for another book.

As part of my healing process, I had to research my lineage. I never knew there was so much healing power in understanding your family history. This process revealed generational patterns that were being repeated—some good and some bad. A few examples of patterns that can be passed down or learned to which many of us can relate include divorce, addictions, having children out of wedlock, and some form of abuse.

My transformation started to evolve when I realized I did not like being vulnerable, which in my opinion at that time was a sign of weakness. I secretly regretted not effectively communicating my own needs to others. Instead of saying "no" or setting boundaries, I did what people needed me to do. Although I would feel frustrated, my need to be viewed as strong caused me not to share my feelings. Sometimes it was easier to walk away. Counseling helped me realize that I created a false reality for the people in my life by appearing to be able to handle everything. I wanted to appear strong and perfect no matter what, even if it was costing me my authenticity.

The self-fulfilling prophecy is real. We have heard that we can simply reframe our belief system by making confessions. When the mind and heart are broken or cluttered, I don't care how many scriptures you memorize or how many positive affirmations you write, you will still believe those negative thoughts. Those negative thoughts will be masked by the positive words. Your mind will battle itself, and you will lose every time.

The only way you can change what you believe about yourself is to adjust your belief system by decluttering your mind first. I believe counseling is the best first step. I personally use 4 R's to continually renew my mind. Counseling has taught me to get *revived, recharged, redirected,* and *released.*

Revive is when I got my fight back. I found myself shrinking back instead of showing up. Counseling elevated my mindset and increased my self-awareness. Did you know that many organizations offer counseling through Employee Assistance Programs (EAP) and insurance plans? This means you might not have to pay for a few sessions. We all like free, right?

Recharge. After getting my fight back, I was willing to do the work toward my healing. Oftentimes, we do not want to invest in ourselves. But we have to get plugged in to the right sources to help us fulfill our destiny. Take inventory of where you are wasting time in your life. To whom and what should you be saying "no"?

Redirect is when I started taking an inventory of the people I had in my life, the paths I was charting, and the decisions I was making. I realized I had to think in terms of addition and subtraction. Who do you need to add and remove from your life to get to your destiny?

Release was the pivotal moment in my life. I realized I did not need a degree to carry out God's plan for my life.

However, it did serve a purpose. It has allowed me the opportunity to share my story and educational knowledge to help heal men and women so they can see their worth in the workplace and in their personal lives. What story do you need to share to help others get healed?

Spiritual counseling was my saving grace. It has become a part of my self-care regimen. I know counseling is taboo because it is only for crazy people, right? Well, call me crazy. But I guarantee if you make counseling a part of your healing process and stick with it, you will have the strength to walk in your God-given purpose and S.T.A.Y. ™ true to you. When you S.T.A.Y. ™, you:

- Stand in your power unapologetically;

- Take control of your thoughts and actions;

- Assess whose help you need; and,

- Yield to the authenticity of you.

Always remember:

"God knows the thoughts and plans he has for you. They are plans to prosper you, not to harm you. Plans to give you a hope for your future."
—Jeremiah 29:11

Real Love

Gail Lee Gardner

GIFT:
SELF-LOVE

Sometimes it is possible to go through life challenges that make you feel worthless to a point of giving up, living with regrets, and even hating yourself. After going through a dysfunctional marriage that led to divorce and having faced two counts of felony charges that separated me from my children, going through a period of not knowing my purpose was inevitable. However, it took a lot of courage and confidence to face my challenges, and learning to love myself first has served an instrumental purpose in helping me become what I am today.

My past experiences make me perfectly understand exactly how you are feeling when you say you are not sure about self and many other life challenges we face as women. I use my personal experiences to help you find your strongest attributes and use them to build a greater version of you. By helping you discover your hidden potential, I help you discover who you really are, and in the long run, develop an unshakable self-confidence.

DEVELOPING AND ATTRACTING LOVE

The experience of going through a dysfunctional marriage is not easy, and for anyone who has gone through the same, you can testify that it makes you question love. You go through a series of thoughts trying to figure out what you did wrong. You blame yourself for so much and imagine all the things you could have done right. As I experienced, these episodes don't make things better unless you make a decision to do better and develop a sense of self-worth in the midst of it.

Unlike the laws of physics, whereby opposites attract, nature has a way of giving us exactly what we are. In short, you will attract what you are. If you are a positive-minded person and love yourself a lot, you are going to attract exactly that. People around you will see you in a positive manner and are more likely to love you back. But if you are negative and don't love yourself, well, don't expect to get love from those around you. After learning this, I started being more positive and loving myself despite everything I was going through.

USING THE LIFE LEMONS TO MAKE LEMONADE

My plight didn't end with divorce or being separated from my children, a predicament that further sent me into agony. After the judge dropped both felony charges and I was able to be back with my children, I knew I had to change for the better and start making better decisions in my life. I knew I needed to become a better mother, a better woman, a better daughter, and a better sister. By doing so, I've embraced my past challenges and discovered my purpose along my journey of self-discovery and have taken what I've learned to help other women.

Through my journey, I read a lot of self-help and inspirational books that helped me become a greater version of myself. My perception of life changed from one of not accepting challenges to embracing the fact that our challenges exist to help us win by learning from them. Deep down, I knew these challenges were preparing me for greatness.

Sometimes you may feel like life is becoming so much of a burden that you lose your faith and lose sight of the big picture. At such moments, you are supposed to trust in God more than ever before, knowing that He is preparing you for something better. I also learned that some of these challenges come as a test to see whether you are ready to handle the greater things life has in store for you.

DEVELOPING SELF-CONFIDENCE AND REALIZING MY POTENTIAL

During my children's early childhood, the Parent Leadership Institute helped parents of the Cincinnati Public Schools to come up with programs that advocated for the education system. I was actively involved in the system and enriched the lives of young girls between the ages of nine and twelve. There came a time when I had to understand the root cause of why women do what we do so that I could better empower young women.

The principal suggested I be a role model for the girls. At that point, I already had a plan to work with both genders, helping six graders with math. At first, I was upset because here I am wanting to address what I saw as a need, and the principal wanted me to do something completely different. But I surrendered to the idea. It took the community to help me create Blossoms, an after-school program. The program came to be a success and was later changed into a tax-exempt organization.

Sometimes when you are expecting a breakthrough after so much struggle, it is easy to be taken aback by rejections. Through personal experience, I learned that what you may want may not add up to what God has planned for you. You will need to practice surrendering and becoming obedient and gaining more faith and self-confidence. The road to realizing your true potential is not always going to be smooth. However, if you maintain your faith and stay focused on your goals, you will get there.

SACRIFICING IS PART OF REACHING YOUR POTENTIAL

At the time I started the Blossoms program, I was working full-time at our local hospital. I stepped out on faith and resigned. This left me with no income. However, I bear witness to the fact that when you take care of the universe, the universe will take care of you. Of course, I utilized local resources and learned how to be creative. I didn't have a mobile phone, and I was using services like Google voice. There is power in being broke because you are forced to be creative and find multiple ways to make it work.

Later, I felt an urge to convert Blossoms from a free service after-school program into a tax-exempt organization. This forced me to go back to work again so I could fund what I needed for the business and take care of my family. Since I was working full-time, I found myself not being able to operate my organization. There was a moment when I thought about getting rid of the business because it was hard for me to find committed volunteers to assist with the day-to-day operations.

Instead of quitting, I pushed through. The fact that I could understand the challenges the girls faced made me want to keep going. It might seem like I went too far while pushing to realize my dreams, but the truth is that sometimes sacrifices are necessary if you are going to live up to your dreams. If you are willing to get something, you must be ready to face a lot of challenges. The only thing that will make you sail through is believing in yourself.

REAPING THE FRUITS

Although at first it seemed like I didn't know who I was, allowing someone to identify my natural talents and gifts and reading self-help and inspirational books helped me to grow. I also unveiled a passion in me for helping others who might be facing the same challenges I did. I can tell you that no matter how bad things get, losing your faith should not be an option.

Always remember that life only gets better. As long as you have confidence in your capabilities, you will definitely make it out smiling. Today, I'm actively involved in empowering women by teaching them to love themselves and invest in themselves. Using my past experiences, I am able to bring hope to those who have lost it and give them the courage to keep pushing even when things don't seem to be working.

Your Passion Is Your Therapy

A FEMALE VETERAN'S PERSPECTIVE

Tevyka Heyward

GIFT:
SELF-LOVE

Finding something that brings you pure joy can also be the one thing that brings you out of your darkest moments.

If there is any lesson I openly share with others it's how I've learned to love and take care of myself. The journey I've taken through anxiety, depression, and PTSD allowed me to go from a person who was "suffering" to a person who lives life on her own terms. If you live with any type of emotional, mental, physical, or spiritual distress, my hope is that reading my perspective on the issue encourages you to see the light at the end of the tunnel and love yourself thorough the process.

I was officially diagnosed with anxiety, sleep deprivation, depression, and PTSD in 2012, and this was only after my mother had begged me to go to the VA (Veterans

Affairs) due to my insomnia and, for lack of a better term, emotional breakdowns. The catalyst had been an unexpected break from my significant other of five years and being unemployed for a little over eight months, all while doing my best to finish my degree and not become homeless. Now at this point some may think, "Okay, big deal; you can recover from a breakup. Unemployment for eight months? There are people who go unemployed for eight years. And there are plenty of people who go to school while still being functioning adults." While I agree in some respects, let me be clear in saying that this timeframe was more like the straw that broke the camel's back than it was the beginning of a struggle.

Looking back, I would have to say my anxiety and depression came from a very hard time for my immediate family. Between 1992 and 1993 we (my baby brother, my dad, and I) almost lost my mother to aneurysms. She had three to be exact. I was about 10, and my brother was three. My dad had just retired from the Army and was driving trucks. We were all adjusting to civilian life on an island in South Carolina. Personally, I was adjusting to being around my stepfather's family, a new school where the kids made fun of how I spoke and the fact that I liked to read, mosquitos, heat, and humidity. Let's just say I was not a happy camper. I wanted to be anywhere but there—maybe Cleveland with my grandparents or New York with my aunt or uncle—anywhere I could feel normal again, normal in the eyes of a 10-year-old. There were even times where I had outbursts and told my mother I hated her for bringing us here and wished she was dead. And then... she almost died.

To be honest, once my mom got sick, a lot of the other stuff didn't matter. My new concern was "Will my mommy ever come back? Will she be herself? Who will take care of us until she does come back? What if she doesn't? How long do I have to deal with all these people in and out of the house telling us what to do?" The day my grandmother showed up, I was so relieved. She was my comfort, my hero, my familiar. What a blessing she was and still is. My mother recovered in ways the doctors said she never would, and just in time, because not too long after my mother returned home, our family was struck with another emergency. My aunt in New York had been rushed to the hospital for aneurysms. I truly believe this is where a lot of my anxiety and sleep deprivation came from. I was worried my family was falling apart and that any night I'd go to bed, I would wake up and someone would be gone forever, not just in a hospital for weeks and months on end.

Through adolescence, my relationship with my mother was interesting to say the least. I had gone from being her sidekick to becoming a part of her caregiving team. I was second woman of the house, taking care of my baby brother, the cooking, and the cleaning. I was also dealing with kids at school talking about my momma's bald head and scars, plus other mean things kids say when you're growing up and you're not a part of the norm. I held resentment and anger toward my family, as if they had any control over what was playing out. But, deep down, I was hurting and didn't know what I was supposed to do about it; so, I began to hate myself (how I spoke, where I came from) and tried to fit in to avoid being picked on. The only thing that would give me peace would be my poetry and short stories.

Fast forward to 2001. I had graduated high school and enlisted in the Air Force and was on my own for what I believed to be a fulfilling career, but I ran into some issues. I was "too direct" and "intimidating" for some. Regardless of knowing my job, working hard, and volunteering/helping others when I could, I was still told I was wrong one way or another. Sometimes it was my fitness. The Air Force wanted me to weigh a certain amount, regardless of how healthy and active I was. My body type didn't fit their mold, so I'd resort to doing whatever it took to get there, even if it was a temporary, unhealthy fix. There were times I was told I had an attitude and I needed to tone it down a bit. At one point, I had a person refer to me in a meeting as an ABW (Angry Black Woman). For a good bit of my life as an adult woman, I was still being told I wasn't enough. And sadly, I started to believe it. I volunteered for deployments because I believed that maybe if I was in a combat zone working hard, people would appreciate my work more than they'd pick at what they believed to be my faults. Of course, according to those in my inner circle, I was fun, caring, and enjoyable to be around, but most didn't know that when I was alone I was beating myself up for not being perfect. I'd be smiling on the outside but miserable on the inside, and at times, I turned to detrimental behavior to cope—drinking, smoking, and other excessive extra-curricular activities. I busted my butt to ensure that I was as sharp as could be professionally, and when I was off duty, I found other ways to cope with the BS.

Relationships were complicated for me; I would give and give only to find myself with people who would only take. I'd go all in only to be rejected months later because I wasn't good enough for them in one aspect or another. I just wanted someone to love me for me, all of me—outspoken, intelligent, sarcastic, independent, and caring me. Wasn't I worthy of that? I began comparing myself to other people and wondering why they could have something stable and be not so nice people and here I was, being myself, and getting nothing but heartache for it. I had this expectation that I would have a military career and a family by a certain age, just like my mom and so many other women I knew and respected. But after each breakup, I would put my blinders on and dive deep into workaholic mode, trying to fill the space with work instead of dealing with myself on an intimate level.

I began to focus so much on my career that relationships became a secondary need for me. My mindset was that I didn't have time for all that mushy stuff anymore, I had to advance in my military career. A career-first mindset led me to the only regret I truly have in my life—forfeiting the opportunity to be a mother. I got pregnant unexpectedly during a period when I had submitted my package to do a job change, something that would require me to be gone often, work long hours, and go through a good bit of physical training. The father and I were actually pretty good friends. He was a nice guy, we had a lot in common, and he had no qualms about my personality or work ethic. When I found out I was pregnant, I saw it as a problem and not as a blessing. I wasn't married, we were both trying to make career changes, and there were some major cultural differences that would have to be addressed. By the time I told him I was pregnant, I had already thought it through and made the decision that I was not going to be a mother. I was in no way, shape, or form ready to be a parent or deal with the repercussions that came with this particular pregnancy. I wanted to focus on my career and do more for myself. The truth is I didn't believe any of those things. I was just afraid he'd bounce and leave me to raise a child on my own. Having been a product of this very situation and seeing what my own mother went through before marrying my stepfather, I wasn't down, and I refused to be hurt again. To my surprise, he didn't want me to have an abortion, but he made it clear that it was my body and my choice. While I respect him for that, there are times when I wish he had talked me out of it. I say this is my biggest regret and recognize that this is where a good bit of my depression comes from. Not that I don't believe in a right to choose. And I know my achievements to date would be completely different had I not made the decision I made. But I do regret not handling the entire situation better. I always told myself I gave up family for career, and it was the best thing because I probably wouldn't have been a good, present, and loving mother because I was still so into what I wanted to do for my career. And then there's how I treated the father. He hadn't done anything wrong. He gave me exactly what I wanted, and I turned on him emotionally. I felt that once I opened up about my situation and what I had done, everyone who knew me would be disappointed and ashamed.

At this point, the self-loathing, self-hate, and negative thinking about not ever being worthy for anyone again came into play. My state of mind leaked into my work performance. All the while, I felt like my entire world was coming down on me all at once.

I was also dealing with my experiences from my two Iraq deployments. Being that the two locations were extremely active, when I returned home, I did my best to suppress some of the incidents we had experienced. But many times, they would replay over and over, just as if it were happening all over again. With so much going on and not having the best interactions with a good bit of the male upper management, I decided it was time to leave my military career behind and find something else—perhaps finish my degree and get a job in a field I truly loved, not just one in which I was pretty well-versed. So, when it was time to re-enlist, I opted for an honorable discharge instead. I needed to have a second go at life as adult. I was dating again and found someone with whom I believed I shared a lot in common. In hindsight, I did the opposite of what I set out to do in being with him. I suppressed a lot of my own views and wants to make him happy just to have someone around. The relationship had its ups and downs, and oftentimes, I believed I had to do whatever it took to make this relationship work because I didn't want to be a failure. I stopped putting my own needs first and took on caring for him and his needs. A good bit of our time was spent long-distance while I was contracting overseas, so we never really got to understand each other outside of two weeks here and there. Just when I thought we would have the time to do so, he decided he needed to get his life right with God... without me. Ouch. At this point, I had the "failed again" mindset and didn't know what else to do. I had taken the option to come home from my contracting job to be with him, and he had decided that that was not what he wanted. This is when I had an emotional breakdown. I didn't leave the apartment I shared with my best friend for almost two weeks, I was struggling to focus in school, and I kept getting rejection after rejection for employment. For someone who had been independent for so long, I was now having to depend on others for assistance. At times, I would be so overwhelmed with emotion and tasks that I'd just shut down and do nothing. Then my mother talked to me one day, and in so many different ways told me to get it together. She gave me a list of things to do, which I'll share with you:

- Do something you enjoy for a few minutes out of each day. (She said, "You were so good at short stories, why don't you try that?")

- Journal your feelings, on good days and bad days, and look at what you can do to improve.

- Be honest with yourself and with others around you regarding how you feel.

- And last but not least (and she said this in her firm yet loving motherly tone), get some help!

I realized at that point that I had nothing to lose, so, I created my first blog. The blog I created was about starting over as a veteran and the avenues I took to get through my days, including some of my shenanigans with my best friend and new experiences with my new friends. The more I wrote and shared, the more I felt a weight being lifted.

Going to the VA for help meant having to be humble and listen to a human being who didn't know me from Adam. I was required to do the work to improve upon myself. There was a lot of crying, a lot of writing, a lot of cussing, and a lot of prayers. I was determined to find a way to love myself and focus on me instead of what everyone else thought of me. Of course, the VA didn't instill the self-love or appreciation for my unique outlook on life, but what it did do was open my eyes and my heart to possibilities and the understanding that as a human being I'm not supposed to be perfect. I was able to come out of my shell and look for ways to be more social again. The blog helped with that as well. I began to interact with women of the same mindset, same goals, and same creative aspirations. I saw so much of myself in them that I was driven to do more and know more about their journey. In turn, I found I could be myself without judgment. The more positive interactions I had, the braver I felt to be myself again—direct, intelligent, independent, funny, nerdy me. My feelings and negative talk to myself began to change. I didn't have to, nor would I ever again, change who I was to make anyone else happy. If I couldn't be appreciated for all the uniqueness I embodied, did a person really deserve my time? It was necessary for me to embrace everything I had experienced and with which I had been challenged, good or bad, own up to life, and decide what truly makes me happy.

My passion for writing, helping others, and travel took a front seat in my life. I filled my weekends working events at a friend's spa. I'd plan trips, even if it was to go see my family. I'd make my own body butters and lip balms to give away to friends as I learned here and there about aromatherapy and holistic care. All in all, what I realized was that I was my own form of therapy and that I could heal by feeding positivity into myself and being selective of what thoughts and actions I accepted as truth. My perspective on life changed. Of course I was worthy of being loved, having a family, and still having a great career and life; all I had to do was remember it didn't have to be on anyone else's terms but my own. Over time, I've run into people, some veterans, especially women, who've had similar stories to mine, and we discus where they may be on their journey to discovery. I am now in a position to remind others of the importance of loving themselves as they are and knowing where they want to grow. While some situations or incidents are inevitable, you don't have to allow them to negatively mold you into someone you are not. Let your passions be your therapy when you are down and let them remind you of how freaking awesome and unique you are. Every single one of us on this planet has a purpose. Letting it be stifled to please others or fit in is a waste of whatever purpose you have here on this earth.

From Blissful Self-Hatred to Conscious Self-Love

Ama Nzinga White

Self-love: "regard for one's own well-being and happiness." At least that is how dictionary.com has defined the term. For me, its meaning goes much deeper. Self-love is not only having regard for my well-being, but also for my true culture via knowledge of self. My true culture, which has been stripped away from me, *should* be the very thing that defines me. Wouldn't anyone who has regard for their well-being be concerned with the culture that has brought forth their ancestors from whom they came? The perfect Afrikan proverb to describe this action would be Sankofa, which means "It is okay to go back for which you have forgotten."

A year ago, my baba said to me, "Nzinga, you are your ancestors projected into the future, which means you are living your ancestors eternal life!" Those words came to me at such a perfect time in my life. Just a few short years ago, I wouldn't have known how to receive those words. Let me take you back to my dark times of unknowingly hating myself.

It started as early as three years of age (and maybe before); I boldly informed my mother that I was going to marry a white man. And not that there's anything wrong with marrying white men; but why, at such a young age, had I already determined that I wanted to spend the rest of my life with a man who held no representation of what my father looked like? It could've been many things, but I attribute the circumstances of my parents' divorce to my thought pattern at such a young age. Even though I wasn't old enough to properly convey my emotions through those tough times my mother and father went through, it still had an effect on me.

As I grew older, mass media only further solidified my blissful self-hate through its black inferiority propaganda. Every time I turned on the television, I saw black people only being portrayed in negative positions. Although there were some good influences on television, such as *The Cosby Show*, they weren't enough to overshadow the negative stereotypes. I remember thinking, "Why do 'these people' have to act so horribly? They are tarnishing my reputation before I even get a chance to speak for myself!" So, I did everything in my power to become a "proper" citizen (or more like assimilate to the dominant culture). I wanted to set myself apart from "other black people." In school, the books I read increased my desires to have been born of a different race. While I was processing these experiences, I was pushing my true self deep into this mental denial vault I had unknowingly created.

As I moved through high school, I suffered from low self-esteem and became sexually active. I was looking for love in all the wrong places, continuously pushing myself deeper into that vault. My desire to be with a white man only grew stronger, but I hadn't acted upon it. Although I grew up in a racially diverse city (my stepfather was in the military at the time, and we lived in a military town, so I saw interracial couples all the time), I never thought I was good enough for a white man. It wasn't until my second year of university that my childhood dream had come true.

At the age of 19, I was finally married to a white male. He was 11 years my senior and I was elated! "He picked me?!" "What did he see in me?!" "Did all of that 'behaving accordingly' finally pay off?" (Yeah, I was definitely lost when I look back at those years.) My ex-husband was the epitome of your right wing, conservative Christian (through no fault of his own), and I followed suit. I did my best to be the wife that *he* could be proud of, not realizing that there I was again, steadily pushing myself deeper into that vault. In those eight years of marriage, I endured so much pain, joy, laughter, hate, and happiness. I couldn't see it until my marriage was over, but I had grown so much over those long eight years. This is when I began my true journey to transform the self-hate into self-love.

As soon as reality hit me that my marriage was over, it was as if I woke up from a dream. Believe me, the waking up process wasn't all that easy either. It was slow progress full of discomfort and pain. Reclaiming my identity was the goal, but I didn't know where to begin. So, I started with denouncing my Christian affiliation. I had prayed so hard for my marriage not to end that when it did, I blamed God, Jesus, Mary, and all of the disciples of the Bible. Let's just say that I soon came to realize that I "threw the baby out with the bathwater."

Not long after my ex-husband and I separated, I was in the arms of another white male. They say old habits die hard, right? I can truly say that this was a step in the correct direction for me. He was majoring in history and getting his teaching degree to teach in the inner-city schools where he grew up. We had deep discussions on race, and I couldn't believe the words that came out his mouth. I was learning things about the Afrikan story that I never knew and never even thought to look into! The words that kept ringing through my head were, "How does this white boy know more about the Afrikan story (OURSTORY) than I do?" That's when it clicked. I needed to put the effort into learning more about "my story" so I could positively affect my future and the generations to come. So in my search, he helped me to find capoeira (an Afrikan-Brazilian martial art), but he and I both knew that our time had come to an end and we broke it off.

Not long afterwards, I ended up dating a handsome black man. And boooooyyyy, did he take me for the cultural ride of my life! For privacy's sake, we'll call him Charles. Charles and I both shared capoeira, but his main purpose in my life was to teach me invaluable life lessons pertaining to my Afrikan culture. I like to refer to those lessons as "healthy pies of truth slammed in my face." So the first thing that had to be done was to destroy the mental denial vault I had created. It was time to unlock it and clean it out. Those moments were the darkest moments of my life.

For example, I had to acknowledge that I had married my ex-husband because of the perceived "white privilege" that I had temporarily acquired. Not an easy feat! I went through a steep learning curve about the realities of racism and so-called white supremacy. No religion to hold my hand, just Charles, who eventually saw that my traumas were too much for him to take on without harming himself. When Charles and I broke up, I realized that the pendulum had swung from one end to another. I went from right-wing, Christian conservative to black is beautiful, power to the people, black fist in the air.

Although it didn't work out for the two of us, Charles did teach me a great deal about myself. I was with him when I took an interest in genealogy after he introduced me to Marcus Garvey's quote, "A people without the knowledge of their past history, origin and culture is like a tree without roots." This is where I began to acknowledge myself as a beautiful black woman (all the while, still searching for womanhood, for the journey is never over). Now that pendulum is slowly swinging toward being centered.

I have a baba and mama who have taken me on as the daughter they never had, and I'm truly grateful for them. They help me run a program called the Ivan Van Sertima Cultural Circles (created by Anthony T. Browder). This program is based on learning about the Nile Valley Civilizations and is run under a company I created called the Afrikan Centered Institute. These study groups have been the primary source of helping me to piece my identity back together so that I may better serve my people.

My baba and mama also helped me to recognize the importance of the foods we eat. They sit on the board of the nonprofit that I recently founded called THINKers, Inc. We are building it from the ground up to help our people with eating healthy to reflect what Imhotep said: "Let your food be your medicine and your medicine be your food."

If there's one thing you remember from my story, remember "You are your ancestors projected into the future, which means you are living your ancestors eternal life!" What are you doing to honor their lives?

Acknowledgments

This book is for you. Perfect, amazing, brilliant, and resilient you.

Please know that everything that has happened *to* you has really happened *for* you so you can heal and help others.

When you choose that perspective, you can use your life lessons as a testament to your powerful journey.

Thank you for being you!

Sources

Unless otherwise indicated, scripture quotations are from the Holy Bible, King James Version. All rights reserved.

Scriptures marked AMP are taken from the Amplified Version®. Copyright © 2015 by The Lockman Foundation. All rights reserved.

Scriptures marked NASB are taken from the New American Standard Bible®. Copyright © 1960, 1962, 1963, 1968, 1971, 1972, 1973, 1975, 1977, 1995 by The Lockman Foundation. Used by permission.

Scriptures marked NIV are taken from the New International Version®. Copyright © 1973, 1978, 1984, 2011 by Biblica, Inc.™. All rights reserved.

Scriptures marked NKJV are taken from the New King James Version®. Copyright © 1982 by Thomas Nelson. All rights reserved.

Scriptures marked TLB are taken from The Living Bible copyright © 1971 by Tyndale House Foundation. Used by permission of Tyndale House Publishers Inc., Carol Stream, Illinois 60188.

About the Authors

Evelyn Ratcliffe studied and performed in many local dance companies in the Valley of the Sun during her youth, including a local performance with the Dance Theatre of Harlem and Pope John Paul II. Her time has been dedicated to several philanthropic projects close to her heart. She has been a Girl Scout troop leader and an executive councilmember for Job's Daughters Bethel 22 Arizona. Evelyn currently serves on the board of directors of the HIKE Fund Inc. (The Hearing-Impaired Kids Endowment), which provides hearing aids to children who cannot otherwise afford them.

She can be found exploring, trying new restaurants, taking in local art, traveling, and making a mean quesadilla when not launching another project! Currently, she is a consultant at Rodan + Fields and a branch president at The Sophisticates Women's Networking Organization.

To connect, email her at
evelyn.a.ratcliffe@gmail.com

Ruby Mabry is a bestselling author, CEO of mental health facilities, thought leader, and coach. She is the founder of the Live on Purpose Movement, where she unites, inspires, and empowers women to live their true purpose in life, professionally and personally.

Learn more at
www.LiveOnPurposeMastermind.com

Sabrina R. Dean, MSA, BSN, RN, with more than 20 years' experience as a registered nurse and a highly motivated, results-driven executive of healthcare management, has a master of science in healthcare administration and a bachelor of science in nursing. She is pursuing her doctorate of business in healthcare administration. She is the co-founder of the African American Women Giving Circle of Dayton, OH, and a founding member of the American Heart Association Circle of Red leadership group. Sabrina's purpose in life is to assist others to live a healthy and fulfilling life. She has effectively influenced, supported, and encouraged colleagues, employees, and families in the community. Sabrina is a smooth jazz listener and travels abroad.

To connect, email her at
preferrednotary@aol.com

Shirley Jean Bazemore is a bestselling co-author of *Souled Out* and a motivational speaker. She was one of the spotlight authors for Delilah Cordova, International Marketing Expert. She resides in Greenville, North Carolina. Shirley retired from East Carolina University with 30 years of experience as an enforcement supervisor. She graduated from Elizabeth City State University with bachelor of science in criminal justice. Her accomplishments from East Carolina University include the African American First Award, Business Service Quest for Excellence Award for positive leadership in the department, East Carolina University Chancellor's Award Synergy for teamwork, and Outstanding Employee Performance Award. She serves as the Staff Senate. Her professional training includes a Certificate in Leadership from East Carolina University, a management course at Rockhurst University, and the Supervision Institute Training Program at International Parking Institute for Customer Service.

To connect, email her at
proverbsw17@gmail.com

Tammie S. Kincaid is a two-time cancer survivor, widow, mother of two boys, and former educator and school counselor. From a young age, Tammie has always had the gift of talking and motivating others. Through her experiences as a lymphoma (2004) and breast cancer (2006) survivor and becoming a widow at the age of 38, she has helped others on their journeys through cancer or the loss of a loved one. She has spoken at several cancer awareness events. Almost one year after the passing of her husband, she had her first speaking engagement as a widow. Her passion is to help others through their circumstances so that they can succeed in life. Her mission is to help others see that they too can survive. She has a bachelor's degree in early childhood education and master's degree in school counseling.

To connect, email her at
TammieKincaid@hotmail.com

Bob Rodgers serves as the CEO of Street Grace, bringing more than 30 years of corporate, nonprofit leadership, and team development experience to this role.

Street Grace is a faith-driven organization that engages faith, business, and community leaders to end domestic minor sex trafficking (DMST) throughout the United States. DMST refers to sexual activity in which there is a promise of the exchange of something of value to a child or another person(s) for sex with that child.

Street Grace mobilizes community resources—financial, human, and material—to fight DMST through awareness, empowerment, and engagement.

To connect, email him at
bob@streetgrace.org

Claudia Wair works as a technical writer and editor. After getting tired of saying "what if?" she finally let go of self-doubt and began pursuing her dream of writing fiction. Now her short stories appear in print and online, and she joyfully continues to hone her craft.

To reach her goals, Claudia developed a journaling method that helped her maintain a positive outlook, take concrete action, and stay motivated when faced with obstacles. She's creating a workbook using this method to help others reach their goals. *Your M.A.P. to Success: 10 Minutes a Day to Navigate the Path to Your Goals* will be available in 2018.

Learn more at
claudiawair.com

Laura Bella is the founder and president of Laura Bella International LLC, an organization dedicated to enriching and empowering the lives of others throughout the world. A lifestyle coach, inspirational speaker, author, model, and vocalist crowned Ms. Plus America 2006-2007, Laura is also the winner of six international awards in modeling, singing, and acting.

Laura is dedicated to coaching and mentoring individuals who desire to achieve self-love. Through her co-authored book, *Woman of Purpose, Power and Passion: An Anthology of Hope & Direction*, she has shared her stories of self-transformation and overcoming self-defeat. Laura is also the creator of international affirmation CDs: *Empowering Affirmations* and *Leadership Affirmations*.

Laura received her bachelor of arts from Columbia College Chicago. She is a certified NLP and is a PMP certification eligible senior project management consultant. Laura is also a licensed life and health insurance agent, and a volunteer vocal singer at Saddleback Church, Lake Forest.

Learn more at
www.LauraBellaInt.com

Millicent Martin Poole is a speaker, bestselling author, training executive, and founder of Upgrade Your Life. Millicent has spoken at corporations, conferences, churches, and women's retreats and has been a featured guest on national podcasts, radio, and TV shows.

Millicent is the author of *What Are You Really Running From?*, a nonfiction book on life lessons learned from the historical Egyptian slave, Hagar. In her latest book, *Be the Answer NOW,* an Amazon bestseller, Millicent and eight business women share how they live out their life's calling and what they overcame to finally reach their epiphany.

Millicent is a recognized leader in accounting and corporate training. She earned her master's degree from Dallas Theological Seminary and her MBA and BS degree in accounting from Alabama A&M University.

Millicent's authenticity and talent for bringing out the best in others has led to her becoming a popular speaker at corporate and church events.

To connect, email her at
poole.millicent@gmail.com

Dr. Jamie Hardy, PharmD, BCPS, MS, is an experienced and well-respected board-certified pharmacist who is also known as The Lifestyle Pharmacist®. She holds a doctor of pharmacy degree, master of science in pharmacy leadership, and board certification in pharmacotherapy. She is a graduate of the ASHP Pharmacy Leadership Academy and The Medical Mogul Academy. As a highly sought-after speaker, bestselling author, and health correspondent, she has been featured in numerous radio, print, and digital outlets. She is a two-time finalist for Best Black Pharmacist in Memphis.

Dr. Jamie is the founder and chief lifestyle curator of Innovative Wellness LLC, a lifestyle company that coaches women to be fit, fabulous, and fulfilled without prescribed pills. Through her videos, books, and programs, she equips them with the tools necessary to exercise, find balance, eat healthier, and effectively manage stress.

Learn more at
www.DrJamieHardy.com

Lisa L. Pena is a seasoned early childhood education leader with more than 25 years of experience. She is the founder of Jamon Montessori Day School and Jamon Foundation.

Lisa owns the only African American Montessori school in the Washington, D.C. area. She conducts coaching at Stepping Stone Homeless Shelter, is an early childhood accreditation specialist for the state of Maryland, and runs a 5K race (Logan's Run).

Lisa conducted a teacher's training workshop in Tempe, West Africa, and presented at the Oxford University Roundtable of ECE. Her philanthropic landscape has included serving on the Boards of Jamon Education Foundation, Lloyd D. Smith Foundation, and W+wINgs.

Lisa received her BA from Hampton University, her masters of education from Loyola College, and her AMI Montessori Certification from the Washington Montessori Institute.

Lisa currently resides in Chevy Chase, Maryland, and is the proud parent of three children ages 26, 25, and 20.

Learn more at
www.LisaLMiller.org

Makena Gargonnu is a celebrity event producer well known for her productions *Conscious Comedy Explosion!* as seen on NBC News and *San Diego Living* as seen on The CW. She is the recipient of the 2013 San Diego Prestige Promoter of the Year Award.

She has been in the comedy industry as a producer for 12 years. Her most successful production, *Conscious Comedy Explosion!*, has been sharing the positive and conscience side of comedy since December 2005 and is taking the comedy world to another level. She believes that it's time for audiences across the country to see more positively influenced comedy shows that are clean, classy, and uplifting.

Her mission is to continue to coordinate culturally centered workshops, educational events, and personal gatherings to embrace cultural diversity and social consciousness. She knows her calling is to transform lives through events that bring joy, happiness and solutions to empower the heartbeat of the world.

To connect, email her at
makena.gargonnu@gmail.com

Paula Dezzutti Hewlette (Pixie Paula), from Charleston, SC, is the CEO of Local Choice Spirits, a family-run award-winning brand development and distribution platform combining the strength of super premium spirits with top-notch celebrity artists and a pioneering loyalty initiative that is a game changer in cause marketing.

Paula spent decades as an expert in the financial and tax planning field before becoming a founding investor and director on the board of a cutting-edge technology company. Her worldwide connections over the last several years have resulted in her being featured in *USA Today Magazine*, *The Huffington Post*, *INC Magazine*, *Yahoo Finance*, *Dow Jones Market Watch*, *Whiskey Passion Magazine*, *Entrepreneur Mind World*, and more. She has spoken at The American Distilling Conference, The American Beverage Consortium, The Los Angeles Brand Innovation Summit, The Confidence Factor for Women and the Wells Luxury Group and has been featured on numerous radio spots.

To connect, email her at
paula@localchoice.us

Renay L. Butler, The Lifeover Coach, is a native Washingtonian and graduate of Morgan State University. She holds a BS in information science & systems. She is a speaker, an award-winning business owner, and an IT professional. She is a member of Alpha Kappa Alpha Sorority, Inc., The Project Management Institute, The National Association for the Advancement of Colored People, and The Prince George's County Women's Bureau. She is the founder of Goal Grinders, Inc., a non-profit organization that teaches children entrepreneurial and leadership skills.

Renay spent the majority of her career as a project manager leading diverse teams and managing multi-million-dollar projects. For the past 15 years, Renay and her team have provided comprehensive business solutions and products that help start or grow your business, identify your niche, expand your customer base, and increase sales through targeted marketing.

Learn more at
www.thelifeovercoach.com

Curtis Venters, widely known as Curtis V, has been on the hair scene for more than 40 years. He is a master stylist, educator, and advisor for the City College Cosmetology Department. He has also held the position as lead educator for Design Essential distributorship. Curtis V's work has been featured on television and news broadcasts, such as KPIX Channel 5 San Francisco's *People are Talking*. He is a published author, percussionist, songwriter, and spoken word artist with a released CD entitled *RSVP*. Curtis V's work has also been featured in *Essence* as well as on album covers and in fashion shows. Curtis V has received many awards, including Salon of the Year and Hair Salon Presentation of the Year.

Curtis V resides in San Diego and is the humble father of five children and nine grandchildren. Curtis V believes family is the most important thing. He loves dancing and meeting new people.

To connect, email him at
thecurtisv@gmail.com

Heidi Lewis is an author, radio personality, educator, and motivator. She is a sought-after inspirational speaker and teacher. Having experienced the pain and stigma of domestic violence, she was able to discover her voice through her writing. She holds a masters in organizational leadership and is a member of Delta Mu Delta International Honor Society. Recognized as a savvy leader and for her ability to train and mentor leaders, she serves as the Executive Director of PureSpring Institute. A lover of God, Heidi places emphasis on leadership through integrity and personal accountability. She speaks of living free, living holistically, and living out loud through hosting the *In My Father's House* radio broadcast. She provides an avenue for women to find strength and refreshing by hosting the Can I Rest Awhile gathering and the empowerment series, Cupcakes and Conversation.

Her mother is her greatest inspiration. Heidi currently resides in Boston, MA.

To connect, email her at
heidi_lewisivey@yahoo.com

Angela Eugene is the founder of Women RISE with Angie, a women's ministry to refresh, inspire, support, and encourage a network of resourceful information to women-specific issues. Angela became a member of The First Baptist Church of Glen Arden in Upper Marlboro, Maryland in 2008. She has functioned in many capacities throughout her commitment to the Lord in the church and has been a blessing with the wisdom with which God has graced her by leading others and sharing all with which God entreats her. Angela currently serves as a Queen Esther facilitator and has served in the Queen Esther ministry since 2010.

Angela was born on a small military base connected to Ft. Bliss, Texas, and was raised in the Washington, D.C. area. Angela is a human resources professional with experience in various industries. She is married to Tyrone Eugene and has two young adults, Jasmin and Nijel.

Learn more at
angie@womenrisewithangie.org

L. Tomay Douglas, social worker, worth strategist, restorative justice practitioner, trainer, and speaker, is the founder of Brand Me Beautiful Inc. She is deeply committed to inspiring thought leaders, influencers, and service providers (coaches, therapists, and practitioners) who are impacted by abuse, betrayal, and trauma to partner with the power they possess to eliminate shame, embrace truth, and live in victory through a process of activating there powersphere. She facilitates innovative trainings and holistic healing worthshops using evidenced-based and restorative practices to help you experience a beautiful breakthrough. The breakthrough will be reflected by being woke, honoring the power of your voice, standing in your truth, and operating from a winner mentality, thus an overcomer who soars.

L. Tomay's story is rooted in love. Her belief is, "Recovery from pain and trauma isn't an exclusive event, it's inclusive, an absolute possibility for all." As a branded beautiful woman or man, you can rise up and soar.

To connect, email her at
LTomayDouglas@gmail.com

Patricia Gibson is a POWERHOUSE Jersey Girl on the move whose mission is to share the beauty in healthy lifestyle choices through education and empowerment. She is a wife, realtor and military relocation professional, beauty educator, and licensed financial professional in San Diego, California. She is the recipient of the 2015 Naval Submarine Base Kings Bay Military Spouse of the Year Award. She holds a bachelor of science in exercise science/physical education from Norfolk State University.

Patricia volunteered as a local director with the Camden Charlton County Board of Realtors®, an ambassador with the Camden County Chamber of Commerce, and chair of the Social, Cultural, & Membership (SCM) Committee for the San Diego Urban League Young Professionals. She has also served as a volunteer for Hamilton's Heart Foundation and the Family Readiness Group (FRG). She is a member of San Diego's Tasteful Tuesdays planning committee for networking events.

Learn more at
www.blesseddivapreneur.com

Sunshine King is a dedicated activist for disability rights, inclusion for persons with disabilities in entertainment, and health and wellness. Sunshine is the survivor of a brutal domestic violence attack in 2004 by her ex-husband that left her with an incomplete spinal cord injury.

She has turned her tragedy into a passion that enhances the mind and spirit of people in need of help. Her desire to nurture what ails has led her to become an entertainment coach and certified wellness practitioner for various agencies. In 2016, she was invited to "walk" the runway at New York Fashion Week. She later had the opportunity to be the first African American model for Tommy Hilfiger's adult adaptive clothing line. Sunshine has been honored as a double survivor by local organizations and been featured on *Inside Edition, MSN News, AOL News, Story Trender*, and numerous radio interviews in multiple states.

To connect, email her at
sunshine_king@aol.com

Tunisia J. L. Patel is a native Chicagoan who lives in San Diego with her husband. She is a professional business woman with her BA in Christian Counseling and MA in Christian Psychology.

She is the owner of Legacy Life Global, an enterprise that encompasses multiple businesses focusing on empowering the spirit of entrepreneurship through education and support services. Legacy Life Global partners with various successful business influencers to host the online Entre Summit DOMINATE annually in January.

Tunisia is also CEO of GracePro Services, LLC, a digital marketing and administrative agency supporting itinerant speakers, executives, and small business owners both virtually and on site.

As a chaplain, Tunisia enjoys serving the community along with her husband via nonprofit business client Stepping Higher, Inc. in California. You can also find Tunisia in worship at Total Deliverance Worship Center in Spring Valley, California.

Learn more at
www.legacylifeglobal.com

Arlene Foster is a lively, spirited conversationalist who lives to spread joy and laughter among her family and friends. It is only natural that her chosen destination steered her toward the field of communications. She received her bachelor of arts in communication and she has Broadcasting and Diversity Studies certificates. Currently, she is pursuing a master's degree in marketing. She has 21 years of experience in communications as a community relations manager, former radio announcer, and advertising consultant. She is a wife and mother of three. In her quest for purpose and guidance, Arlene realized that her true calling lies in spiritual edification. Her mission is to inspire and encourage others as they explore, discover, and develop their God-given talents so that they may live a purpose-driven life.

To connect, email her at
arlene.foster.5c@gmail.com

Aurea McGarry is an Emmy Award–winning TV show host, producer, director, author, speaker, emcee, and founder of Live Your Legacy Summit and A.M.P–Aurea McGarry Productions. A.M.P is a full-service media company for businesses and nonprofits. She is a frequent TV host for *Atlanta Live*, a cancer and domestic violence sur-THRIVER, and a walking miracle.

Aurea's been featured on over 400 radio shows and dozens of TV shows with audiences in the millions, including *The 700 Club*, *Atlanta & Company*, FOX, PBS, NBC, and *Nite Line*.

As a sought-after speaker, she travels the country inspiring people to live their best legacy, and as a media coach, she teaches business owners how to become the "go-to" celebrity expert in their industry.

Aurea faced many struggles, including the murder of her father, divorce, domestic violence, and cancer. She wrote her autobiography titled *I Won't Survive, I'll Thrive!* about how she overcame them all while staying positive and successful.

Learn more at
www.AureaMcGarry.com

Blaque Diamond is a rare diamond. Her composition sets her apart from other writers of all kinds. Diamond is the author of the *Stacey F.* children's book series. Diamond graduated from Morgan State University School of Social Work, where she earned her BSW and MSW degrees and was an All-American Collegiate Scholar. In addition to writing children's books, she's an advocate for children waiting for foster care/adoption, family restoration, and reunification with their biological parents. She is the 2017 Indie Author Legacy Award Community Champion Legendary Honoree. Diamond has three biological children and raised nine nieces and nephews, five of whom she was granted custody and three of whom she adopted from the NYC foster care system. She resides in Maryland with her children.

To connect, email her at
Blaquediamond357@yahoo.com

Dr. Angela Kenzslowe is a lover of life. She believes we get one life and wants the best life possible. She has a passion for helping others, whether healing emotional trauma, helping launch businesses, or finding peace.

She's explored the world professionally as a soldier, actor, speaker, entrepreneur, business professional, college professor, and clinical psychologist. As a psychologist, she specializes in the treatment of trauma, depression, and anxiety. She was trained by the Department of Defense and founded Purple Heart Behavioral Health, LLC to help service members and civilians.

Additionally, Dr. Kenzslowe earned an MBA and a bachelor's in theatre. She's shared the screen and stage with A-List entertainers. She's been quoted in major publications. She's done original empirical research to move the science of psychology forward. Dr. Kenzslowe believes we should be free to be our true and authentic selves and hopes her contributions to the world make it a better place.

Learn more at
www.DrAngelaKenzslowe.com

Ericka L. McKnight resides in North Carolina. She is a mother of three, five-time bestselling author, philanthropist, and CEO of ELM Realty Firm & ELM School of Real Estate. She is currently the youngest and only African American women to own a real estate school in North and South Carolina with satellite-partnered offices in Georgia and Tennessee. She has obtained numerous awards, including Top Female Entrepreneur of the Year in Charlotte, NC, Homeownership Dream Military Veterans Award, Author of The Year Award from the African American Author Literacy Coalition, and the 10th Annual NAACP Authors Honoree Pavilion.

She has been featured in *Pride Magazine* (the largest African American magazine in the Carolinas), *Huffington Post, Influence Magazine, Forbes*, and many more.

Learn more at
www.silencethenoiseelm.com

Dr. Tabatha Carr, ND, MBA, PMP, is a leading authority in the field of women's health and wellness, focusing on the extremely powerful and effective tools of natural medicine. She is a leading advocate for women using the power of their mind, body, and spirit to bring positive changes to their lives.

Dr. Carr recognizes that women today face many personal challenges that can keep them from living a full life, including issues around weight management, hormonal imbalances, blood sugar imbalances, adrenal fatigue, and more. Dr. Carr specializes in identifying the root causes of a woman's symptoms and partners with her to address these issues, leading to a life of energy, good health, and balance.

When she is not working, Dr. Carr focuses on bringing positive energy to her community. She can be found playing the piano for her church, volunteering at local charities, or doing public speaking.

Learn more at
www.livingandlovinglife.org

Tonia Marie Robinson founded Divas with Purpose and is the creator, executive producer, and television host of *Tonia & Friends*.

Tonia's program celebrates the total diversity of community. The contributions of individuals and groups of all ethnicities and backgrounds are highlighted. The show features such topics as music, fashion politics, art, business, parenting, and more from the people who are bettering our complete community.

A former Miss North Valley, Phoenix, educator, hospice nurse and VA nurse, Tonia speaks on fully living with passion and compassion every moment of your life.

Learn more at
www.toniaandfriendstv.com

Harriette P. Gibbs is a certified special educator, entrepreneur, former host of the blog talk radio show *WOW Inspiration* and author. She was a featured guest on *The Alfreda Love Show* and on *Women to Watch with Jaha Knight*. She is the founder of Harriette Gibbs Inspires LLC and the CEO of the Howard and Elizabeth Caldwell Foundation. Her passion is to inspire and empower women to become Dream Catchers. She also has a passion for assisting parents who have children with special needs.

To connect, email her at
harriette@harrietteinspires.com

Dr. Lisa Guerrant is not your typical life or transformational coach; she is a "creative seeker of fabulousness" and a lover of confidence! Dr. Guerrant has overcome insurmountable odds and learned early in life that if you control your mindset, you can transform yourself and your life, creating endless possibilities. She uses those life lessons to share real-world strategies with her clients to unleash and maximize their personal and professional potential. Dr. Guerrant holds two bachelor's degrees in liberal arts and management, a master's in business administration, and a PhD in education with a specialization in training & performance improvement. Dr. Guerrant also has certifications as a holistic life coach, personal fitness trainer, and master herbalist, allowing her to continue her holistic practices on new levels. She has worked extensively with professionals helping them discover their purpose, gain clarity, and overcome a multitude of obstacles leading to their success.

Learn more at
www.empoweringdivinemindz.com

Wendy Shurelds is a mother, realtor, entrepreneur, and breast cancer survivor. She is the founder and host of the *Many Shades of Pink & Black Health* radio program on kblkradio.com. Wendy is the community resource advocate for Susan G. Komen San Diego Circle of Promise. She is the winner of San Diego Padres 2017 Honorary Bat Girl for her strength in fighting breast cancer and commitment to helping others and the recipient of North San Diego County NAACP Game Changer Award for her outstanding service and devotion in the community. She is an activist for workplace safety after tragically losing her mother in a preventable workplace incident. Wendy received the WWE Survivor Championship Belt for being a champion in the community. Fighting for, educating, and empowering women is Wendy's passion and makes her heart smile.

To connect, email her at
many.shadesofpinkbh@gmail.com

Bonita Owens is a certified life coach and inspirational speaker. She received her certification in professional coaching and energy leadership in 2017 from the Institute for Professional Excellence in Coaching (iPec). She is also a member of Toastmasters International. She holds a bachelor's degree in occupational therapy from Tennessee State University.

Bonita decided to change careers in 2014. She created the Amazing Women Network, where she helps women who want to be more, do more, and have more by supporting them in finding their significance, reclaiming their purpose, and creating an amazing life.

Learn more at
www.amazingwomennetwork.com

Dr. Mia Cowan, **MD, MBA, MA**, aka "Dr. Mia," is among the country's best-known and respected board-certified gynecologists. She travels throughout the world speaking at corporations, conferences, universities, and churches on insights and strategies for improving the quality of life of women struggling with weight gain, fatigue, and sexual dysfunction. Her relatable yet medically sound approach to making lasting lifestyle health changes has earned her the title of "The B3 Specialist" by her colleagues and patients. Dr. Mia is highly sought after by print, online, radio, and TV media outlets to provide a fresh perspective on "experiencing your *B*eauty, *B*alance, and *B*elief to always live well and age beautifully!"

Dr. Mia is a two-time bestselling author and the founder and medical director of MiBella Wellness Center, where she provides superior and compassionate gynecology services to women of all ages with emphasis on prevention and lifelong wellness through hormone balance.

Learn more at
www.MiBellaWellness.com

Chantelle Cotton is a master sales trainer/coach and motivational speaker with over 15 years of sales experience and a proven track record. She teaches entrepreneurs, small business owners, and corporations how to increase their revenue by closing more sales. Her authentic sales approach focuses more on the conversation and relationship building aspect of the sales process versus just sales.

Through the creation of The Luxxe Level Group Sales Training & Business Development Company and the Why Do I Say Yes? program, Chantelle is able to impart wisdom from her lessons learned to audiences across the nation. She is a widely sought-after speaker whose effectiveness is attributed to the fact that she has lived the life about which she speaks. It is through motivational speaking, empowering workshops, leadership conferences, and other events and activities that Chantelle most effectively delivers her wisdom and knowledge by sharing her true-to-life experiences and authentic sales approach.

Learn more at
www.WhyDoISayYes.com

Che Haughton, born in Shreveport, Louisiana, and made in Atlanta, Georgia, is on a journey to empower, educate, encourage, and enlighten everyone! Che has lost a total of 160 pounds through mental healing, diet, and exercise.

Che is a mother to an amazing daughter, Aubrienne. Through the power of social media, Che has established a powerful connection with numerous women and men all over the world by sharing her testimonies, struggles, joys, and pains.

Being a fatherless child, being bullied, and having failed relationships all contributed to her being unhappy and unhealthy at her highest weight of 325 pounds. Through her discovery, she found her purpose. That purpose was to encourage others to get to the root cause of their issues, turn that pain into passion, and live freely.

Che is also the 2017 *Bold Favor Magazine* Wellness Award winner and a contributing health and wellness writer for *Kontrol Magazine*.

Learn more at
www.cheinspires.com

Cynthia McCalister has been a leader in information technology for over 20 years, working at top fortune 100 companies. She holds a master of science degree in information technology management from Colorado Technical University, a bachelor of science degree in electrical engineering from Wright State University, and a wealth of certifications, including Project Management Professional (PMP) and Certified Scrum Master (CSM).

Cynthia started the IT company Quality SAP in 2007. Quality SAP stands for Quality, Service, and Products. Its mission is to support small businesses and give back to the community. It is a certified minority and female-owned business. Quality SAP offers affordable mobile technology platforms, such as the "Key Spot" mobile app (www.keyspotapp.com), used by business owners across the county to share information within the community. Cynthia's motivation is her husband and children. She continuously strives to demonstrate that "anything is possible to achieve with God, a dream, and hard work."

Learn more at
www.qualitysap.com

Dr. Christi Monk received her doctor of management in organizational leadership studies. Her published work is entitled "Workplace Bullying in Search of a Clearer Definition: A Modified Delphi Study." She is an international speaker, trainer, and coach. She founded the Workplace Leadership Institute; The Confidence Suite; and Women with Beauty, Brains, and Boundaries. She has been featured in *Essence Magazine, The Women Business Report, The Happy Black Woman* and *Black Woman CEO* podcasts, *The Sharvette Mitchell Show*, and the National Association for Professional Women. She serves as co-chair of the Women's Leadership Council and on the board of directors for Servant Hearts, Inc. She is a Women's Speak leader who is certified in Workplace Bullying, Change Management, Life Purpose Coaching, Brain-Based Coaching, and Workplace Mediation. Dr. Monk is passionate about helping others find their voice and discovering their purpose so they can walk in their authenticity boldly. She currently resides in Maryland.

Learn more at
www.christimonk.com

Gail Lee Gardner is a soul sparker, mompreneur, educational advocate, and humanitarian. As the founder of the life-changing organization, I AM Blossoms International, she is a catalyst of growth and promise. With humble beauty, Gail is well known for igniting healing fires and developing positive systemic strategies.

In a personal conversation with Gail Lee Gardner, she was asked to recite her personal motto. Boldly and with a faithful conviction, she answered, "Use what you have today to empower tomorrow." She is looking forward to launching her first book and hopes to connect with her audiences both stateside and internationally.

To connect, email her at
Gailinc2@gmail.com

Tevyka "Tee" Heyward is a U.S. Air Force veteran, Army brat, veteran blogger, and advocate for living one's best life chapter by chapter. Between the military and her career after service, she's worked between Iraq and Afghanistan since 2003 and traveled to Africa and hidden gems in the Caribbean. She holds a BS in human services. Tee is known by her family and friends as somewhat of a busybody and student of life. Her blog, *The Phoenix Chronicles*, is geared toward veteran women transitioning into a happy and healthy life after service. She believes that everyone can apply something from her life stories, or what she affectionately refers to as "chronicles," to their lives.

She's a proud godmother and aunt. She loves connecting with fellow veterans, traveling, and cooking.

Learn more at
http://thephoenixchronicles.me

Ama Nzinga White is on an Afrikan-centered journey. After five years of feeling lost in the accounting industry, she needed a change. She realized she was exhausting her energy in the wrong field and for the wrong purpose. Everyone kept telling her "just be yourself," but when she tried, she drew a blank. She didn't know who she was or where she came from. She knew nothing of her story. She thought, "How is one supposed to be themselves if they don't know anything about their past?" She then came across the following quote from Marcus Garvey: "A people without the knowledge of their past history, origin and culture is like a tree without roots," which led her to explore her true culture. One of her newfound duties is to lead people toward Afrikan excellence by giving them knowledge. Another is to lead by example.

To connect, email her at
juelre87@gmail.com

Kim Coles is a beloved actress, comedian, speaker, and teacher most known for her role as an original cast member on the ground-breaking sketch comedy, *In Living Color* and as the lovable Synclaire on the long-running hit Fox series, *Living Single*. In 1998, she became a published author with *I'm Free, but It'll Cost You*, a hilarious guide for frustrated women in the dating scene.

Soon after *Living Single* was cancelled, Kim waded into a deep depression. As her weight increased, her funds decreased. Having lost sight of her self-worth and self-esteem, her survival required a drastic change of mind. The first step was finding a therapist, and the tools gained through therapy flipped her perspective and her life right-side up again. She realized that while she has a phenomenal gift of performance, she also has a spiritual calling to help women access their own gifts, share them with others, and enjoy a more fulfilled life.

Kim has since regained control of her life, married her soulmate, starred in several films and television shows, hosted the BET game show *Pay It Off*, won the inaugural Indie Author Legacy Awards for independent authors, and published *Open Your G.I.F.T.S*, a collaborative book for women in search of a deeper level of satisfaction in their lives.

She is passionate about helping others tell their powerful stories and can help you uncover yours with her course, which you can find at www.loveyourstory.biz

To learn more, visit her website at
www.kimcoles.tv

purposely created
PUBLISHING

CREATING DISTINCTIVE BOOKS
WITH INTENTIONAL RESULTS

We're a collaborative group of creative masterminds
with a mission to produce high-quality books to position
you for monumental success in the marketplace.

Our professional team of writers, editors, designers,
and marketing strategists work closely together to ensure
that every detail of your book is a clear representation
of the message in your writing.

Want to know more?
Write to us at info@publishyourgift.com
or call (888) 949-6228

Discover great books, exclusive offers, and more at
www.PublishYourGift.com

Connect with us on social media

@publishyourgift